THE POLITICAL SYSTEM
OF NAPOLEON III

THE POLITICAL SYSTEM
OF NAPOLEON III

BY

THEODORE ZELDIN
M.A., D.Phil.
*Research Fellow of St. Antony's College
and sometime Scholar of Christ Church
Oxford*

LONDON
MACMILLAN & CO LTD
NEW YORK · ST MARTIN'S PRESS
1958

MACMILLAN AND COMPANY LIMITED
London Bombay Calcutta Madras Melbourne

THE MACMILLAN COMPANY OF CANADA LIMITED
Toronto

ST MARTIN'S PRESS INC
New York

PRINTED IN GREAT BRITAIN

PREFACE

THIS book is based very largely on unpublished sources. The answers to the problems with which it deals could not be found in other books and the author therefore had to spend a good deal of time searching for new material. He was fortunate in finding the private papers of many of the leading figures of the period. It was not simply a question of tracking down their owners, for then he sometimes had to search dusty attics and dark cellars for the documents themselves. The hunt for one manuscript ended in a chalet in the Alps, where, after the strongboxes whose keys had been lost had been forced open in vain, it was discovered lying unguarded on top of a wardrobe. The hunt for one owner began in a clue he picked up from a conversation with a shopkeeper and was not successful until he had followed it up through a whole series of dingy offices of merchants and auctioneers in the narrow back streets of Paris.

The author found valuable material in the public archives as well. Much has remained unused there because it cannot be understood without a very detailed knowledge of the men of the period ; and the conclusions which appear in this book could therefore be drawn only after investigating the affairs of tiny villages and unravelling the intrigues of a vast number of people now totally forgotten. In this way he has used the particularly rich collection of correspondence on the election of 1852, which provides a unique picture of French politics in the nineteenth century. Many documents, however, have been lost or destroyed and there was nothing similar for the rest of the reign. The author, therefore, had the idea of going to the archives of the Post Office and there indeed he found copies of a huge quantity of confidential telegrams, which, though not as full as the missing letters, yet contained much information. When nothing more could be found in Paris, he sought out the archives of the prefects in the provinces and with their aid was able to carry the story to its end and to explain the decline into which Napoleon's political system fell.

He wishes to thank here the descendants of the statesmen of the second empire who most generously allowed him to make use of their private archives and who supplied him with much valuable information and reminiscence: M. and Mme M. Barrois, M. le Comte and Mme la Comtesse de Bertier de Sauvigny, M. J. Buffet and Mme B. Buffet, M. P. de Cassagnac, General Comte de Chambrun, M. le Marquis and Mme la Marquise de Chasseloup-Laubat, Mme Duchon d'Espagny, M. de Forcade la Roquette, M. D. Maître, M. Meynis de Paulin, M. le Comte and Mme la Comtesse A. de Montalembert, M. C. Schneider, M. le Marquis de Talhouet-Roy, Mme Troisier and Mme de Waru. He wishes to thank also the many historians, writers, and others both in England and in France who advised and helped him in the course of his work. He owes more than he can say to many of them, but he hopes they will excuse him from filling several pages with their names, just as he hopes that those he has mentioned will forgive his acknowledging so briefly all the kindness and hospitality they have shown him.

CONTENTS

ABBREVIATIONS IN THE FOOTNOTES

PVCL *Procès-Verbaux des séances du Corps Législatif,* 1852–1865

CRCL *Compte-Rendu des séances du Corps Législatif,* 1852–1860

ACL *Annales du Sénat et du Corps Législatif,* 1861–1870

M.U. *Moniteur universel*

B.N. *Bibliothèque Nationale*

B.N.N.A.Fr. *Bibliothèque Nationale, Nouvelles acquisitions françaises* in the department of manuscripts

A.N. *Archives Nationales*

A.D. *Archives Départementales*

The abbreviation A.N. is not repeated before documents obviously coming from the National Archives and which have an official abbreviated *côte,* viz. F, C., BB.

NOTE ON TRANSLATIONS

The members of the various parliaments in France in the nineteenth century had different titles at different times : *députés, constituants, représentants, membres du corps législatif*. To simplify matters, all these have been translated not 'deputies' (which would be proper only for those who were members of *Chambres des Députés*, and which, in the context of this book, would suggest the parliamentarians of the Orléans monarchy) but 'M.P.s'. This does not, of course, imply that they had the same characteristics or functions as M.P.s in England.

During the second empire, 25 French francs were equal to one pound sterling ; and French money has accordingly been converted on this basis into contemporary English money and not into present-day values.

myth

CHAPTER I

How men survived in politics and how new men entered it

(1814–1870)

MARSHAL BUGEAUD, the conqueror of Algeria, on his return to Paris after his victories, was summoned by King Louis Philippe. 'I wish to have a talk with you,' he said, 'since you are the man who knows Algeria better than anyone else.' The king then proceeded to talk himself without stopping for nearly two hours; after which he shook Bugeaud's hand and said, 'Thank you, I am delighted with the conversation we have had'. Some time later Louis Napoleon, as President of the Republic, summoned Bugeaud likewise. He greeted him with words very similar to Louis Philippe's. He then listened to Bugeaud for two hours without interrupting him and without saying a word. After which he shook his hand and said, as Louis Philippe had done, 'Thank you, I am delighted with the conversation we have had'.[1]

This story illustrates the problem of the second empire. How can one hope to understand a man who spoke so little and who wrote even less? There is no great collection of letters in fifty volumes for him, as there is for Napoleon I, to show not only what his wide aims were in broad outline, but also how far his detailed administration corresponded to them. It is all very well to echo his words that he stood for the peasants, for prosperity or for glory, but the character of his régime cannot be determined merely from his grand generalisations and high-sounding claims. It is more

[1] Ollivier's diary, 7.2.1864.

I

important to know what this régime was than what it said it was.

Now Napoleon could not govern without the co-opera-tion of ministers, administrators and a horde of subordin-ates, who possessed individualities of their own, who left their own stamp on the period and who inevitably influenced the formation and the execution of policy. But who were these men? The Bourbons, it is said, were supported by the aristocracy, the Orléans by the bourgeoisie, the republic by the masses: who then supported the second empire? Much has been written about its general but very little about its officers and its army. The object of this book is to deal with this problem, to discover who these supporters of Napoleon III were and so to show the real foundations of his power. In order to obtain as precise an answer as possible, it will deal more particularly with the members of his parliaments. These men have long languished in obscurity, but through them it will be possible to explain the nature of the Bonapartist party. Through them also it will be possible to see why the second empire came to be transformed from an authoritarian into a liberal govern-ment.

This transformation is one of the most interesting puzzles of the century. In 1852 Napoleon III, having dissolved the National Assembly, became the practically absolute ruler of France. He proclaimed the end of the parliamentary system which the country had practised since the fall of the great Napoleon and which, he asserted, was responsible for bringing it down from its former great heights of glory. He re-established his uncle's organisation of personal government: he would rule through ministers chosen at his pleasure and through pre-fects who would reflect his omnipotence in the provinces in the manner of the proconsuls of ancient Rome. He would nominate the celebrities of his reign to a senate, whose task would be to watch over the maintenance of the constitution and keep things as they were. His civil servants in the council of state would prepare the laws, which would be submitted to a legislature elected by universal suffrage, having the right to reject them, it is true, but with strictly limited powers of amending them and whose debates would be published only in abbreviated and censored form. In two plebiscites the masses confirmed all his acts.

Gradually, however, Napoleon increased the powers of the legislature and by 1870 he appeared to have yielded up the government to it and to have re-established the parliamentary system. Did this represent an abdication on his part before the demands of the growing opposition, an acknowledgement of his failure and an attempt to give up his power in order to keep his throne? Or was it the result of a change of heart? Is the history of his reign the story of his conversion from an autocratic dictator into a disciple of the liberal creed? This book will seek to give the answer.

It is generally assumed that Napoleon III owed his election to power to his name, to the legend his uncle had created, but not to the work of any party of his own, which in 1848 just did not exist. It is well known that after the fall of the second empire a strong Bonapartist party continued to flourish for twenty years. Why was this so? How could it be that the mighty first empire should by contrast disappear, leaving only a few misguided conspirators faithful to its memory?

The answer is to be found in the different ways the two empires fell. In 1870 the whole body of the supporters of the régime were violently expelled and smeared as the collaborators of 'the despot'. A sharp line was drawn between them and those who had not served Napoleon and they were thus made into a party as much by their enemies as by themselves. Something very different happened in

3

1814. Napoleon I was overthrown but his followers were not. They arranged the Bourbon restoration and were absorbed into the new system. Even when they were largely expelled from office as the government moved right, they kept their place in the régime and merely became its left wing. They cast off their Bonapartist slough and emerged transformed as liberals. 'Bonapartist, then liberal,' as Balzac says, 'for by one of the strangest of metamorphoses, the soldiers of Napoleon nearly all became lovers of the constitutional system, Colonel Guiget was during the restoration the natural president of the organising [liberal] committee of Arcis.'[1] In 1830 most of these liberals came into power and changed their name once more, to Orleanists. Hence it was that the Orléans monarchy secured the return of the ashes of Napoleon, built the Invalides to house them and erected his statue in the Place Vendôme. Its parliament paid perpetual homage to his memory; it protested when an M.P. dared to refer to him simply as 'Bonaparte', and infuriated republicans complained in vain that his example was cited too often.[2] It dismissed an official for having led a mob in 1815 to drag a bust of the emperor into the mud.[3] Its House of Peers, which in 1840 tried Louis Napoleon for seeking to overthrow the government, is said to have included no less than 4 ministers, 6 marshals, 56 generals, 14 councillors of state, 19 prefects, 7 ambassadors, and 21 chamberlains of the first empire, and 38 men who had publicly recognised the accession of Napoleon II after the Hundred Days.[4]

It was, however, no paradox that they should condemn

[1] Balzac, *Le Député d'Arcis*, ed. Bouteron and Lognon (1949), 283-4.
[2] M.U. 1847, 841 and M.U. 1841, 1538. The abbreviation M.P. is used throughout this book as the most convenient translation of the various names given to the members of the lower houses of parliament of the nineteenth century : *députés, membres du corps législatif, représentants*, etc. See note on translations on page x.
[3] M. Rousselet, *La Magistrature sous la monarchie de juillet* (1937), 37.
[4] *Aux mânes de l'empereur, la pairie reconnaissante* (1840), Lb (51) 3137. For the meaning of the terms Orleanist, legitimist and republican see below, Chapter XII.

the heir of the emperor. Their position was quite clear. They were 'Napoleonists', not Bonapartists. They were proud of their maker, who was the creator of their titles, their distinctions and frequently of their wealth; they honoured him and they punished those who blasphemed him; but they were satisfied that he should remain among the gods and leave them to govern themselves in peace through their own 'puppet king'. As a senior civil servant said, 'Bonapartism was excited by the sound of the homage done to Napoleonism, and a child came to Boulogne to fail against France as his uncle had failed against England. . . . [Now] that Bonapartism is placed under lock and key in the castle of Ham it is possible to pay perfectly peaceful honours to the personal glory of Napoleon.'[1] Bonapartism, wrote a contemporary, was no longer based, as it was in the first part of the restoration, on loyalty and devotion to the dynasty. 'No member of the former imperial family can today flatter himself that he is the object of the chivalrous cult which the Bertrands, the Lacazes, the Montholons and the Labedoyères formerly professed for their illustrious master. The monarchy of July, by adopting the glories and the misfortunes of the empire, has acquired a right to their loyalty, and it is among the companions at arms of Napoleon or among their sons that Louis Philippe today finds his most declared partisans and his staunchest supporters.'[2]

Louis Napoleon had thus to seek his allies among the opponents of the monarchy, and since he could not base his party on men who were seriously involved in the politics of his day, he had to base it on ideas which appealed to the masses. He advocated universal suffrage against the closed franchise of the monarchy; and as the inevitable ally of the republicans he preached the restoration, not of the empire,

[1] J. Taschereau, *Revue rétrospective* (1848), 140-1.
[2] Gustave de Romand, *De l'état des partis en France* (1839), Lb (51) 2944, 23-5.

but of the consulate and the republic.[1] The revolution of
1848 was a triumph for him and for all the opponents of
Louis Philippe, and not simply for the pure republicans.
The legitimists were offered a seat in the provisional
government; they flocked into the constituent assembly;
and the reaction in the following year was directed almost
as much against them as against the republicans. The
clergy blessed the trees of liberty not from any affection
for the new form of government, but rather because it
meant the end of Louis Philippe's Voltarian system, and
they showed it quite plainly by canvassing for their own
legitimist or clerical candidates at the elections.[2] In the
same way members of the imperial family were elected as
part of the general movement and Louis Napoleon's old
tutor was appointed *commissaire* of the republic in Manche.
The peasants who voted for Louis Napoleon in December
1848 voted a few months later for the reddest republicans,
as though for one and the same cause.

Yet there is a myth that he was elected to the presidency
as the candidate of the opponents of the republic, the 'party
of order', adopted by them as a useful tool to overthrow
the régime which had brought him back to France. In
fact he was not elected because he was their candidate, but
he was their candidate because they saw he was bound to
win. They had no choice in the matter, said Thiers, the
masses were all for him. The size of his majority may have
caused some surprise but his victory was certainly not unexpected.[3] Had the party of order been able to win merely
on the principle of order, Thiers would have stood himself.
'Many of my friends', he wrote, 'want me to accept [the

[1] H. Malo, *Thiers* (1932), 273 ; É. Ollivier, *Le 19 Janvier* (1869), 148 ;
H. Avenel, *Histoire de la presse française* (1900), 373 ; B. Jerrold, *Life of
Napoleon III* (1874), 1. 241-2, 250-1 ; 2. 470 ; Napoleon III, *Œuvres* (1856),
1. 382 ; E. d'Hauterive, *Napoléon III et le prince Napoléon* (1925), 11
and 30.   [2] F(19) 5604.
[3] M.U. 1851, 184 ; Montalembert to Falloux, 12.10.1848, Montalembert papers ; Barada to Thiers, 29.10.1848. B.N.N.A.Fr. 20617 ff. 255-6 ;
Barante, *Souvenirs* (1890–1899), 7. 385.

candidature for the presidency] to oppose a candidature which they regard as detestable, that of Louis Bonaparte. They think, and I think so too, that I alone could be opposed to Bonaparte in the name of the principles of order. But if I can stand against him, I doubt whether I can succeed, at least at present. . . .'[1]

As president, therefore, Napoleon did not represent the party of order. The whole conception of this party is in any case misleading. All governments, even the republic, proclaimed themselves the representatives of the party of order and labelled all opposition as anarchy. All oppositions in their turn called the governments in power tyrants and thieves and announced that they themselves were seeking liberty and order — the two always went together. In 1850 Napoleon said, 'Order for me is not a meaningless word which everyone interprets as he pleases. For me order is the maintenance of what has been freely elected and agreed to by the people, it is the national will triumphant over all factions.'[2] The party of order thus means the party of whoever invokes its name and it is therefore of little value as a description of the basis of Napoleon's power.

A phrase more useful to understanding it, and to understanding the meaning of the revolutions between 1814 and 1870 in general, is 'new men', the universal cry which rose from the victors of every revolution. The parliamentarians and the senior civil servants who had supported the previous government were declared corrupted by their contact with it and their places were taken over by 'new men'. Immediately after every revolution the ministers were besieged by place hunters seeking the booty of victory, very often basing their claims to favour simply on their opposition to the fallen government.[3] And this search for

[1] Bibl. Thiers, Fonds Thiers, 1ère Série, No. 24, f. 60, letter of 17.10.1848.
[2] Napoleon III, *Œuvres*, 3. 133-4.
[3] *E.g.* Ste-Hermine's file (F(1b)I 173(4), letter of 28.7.1848. Mesgrigny, M.P., 15.3.1836 in Rambourgt's file, F(1b)I 172(2).

B

jobs was as much the cause as the result of revolutions. 'The moral disturbance' of the time, said Tocqueville in 1842, was due to this 'growing, unbounded and disordered passion' of the country.[1] Men talked of 'the fever of ambition which devours every head and which excites every mind', as though it was 'impossible to live any longer today outside public employment'.[2] An economist went so far as to claim that there was nothing in these perpetual revolutions but a struggle for place. 'As every place has at least five candidates, and every candidate hopes that a revolution will turn out the actual possessor, above a million of our most active talkers and writers are always agitating to overturn the existing constitution for the purpose of ejecting those who hold its places.'[3]

This is of course an over-simplification which ignores the thousand different motives which cause men to act as they do, but there can be no doubt that revolutions did have this uniform characteristic of putting new men into the administration. Now this was required not simply by the ambition of the victors, but also by two independent circumstances. In 1830, in 1848 and in 1870, just as the kings abdicated without resisting, so likewise their followers retired voluntarily, invoking their loyalty to their sovereign in order to escape being forcibly evicted. The jobs were simply left vacant. Secondly, every government which did not want to be sabotaged in the provinces had to fill the civil service with its supporters, quite apart from the need to reward these supporters. The faithful must be given power to breed yet more faithful. 'If there are no royalists in France,' wrote Chateaubriand in 1815, 'we must make royalists. . . . A bishop, a commanding officer, a prefect, a public prosecutor, a president of a court of martial law, a commander of police, and a commander of the national

[1] M.U. 1842, 108-9.
[2] M.U. 1842, 196-7, speech of Monier de La Sizeranne.
[3] N. Senior, *Conversations with Thiers* (1878), i. 191-2.

guard : let these seven men be for God and the King, and I answer for the rest.' [1]

Looked at in the light of these facts, the careers of the politicians reveal signs of a pattern which makes the meaning of the period clearer. The servants of Napoleon I, the supporters of the Hundred Days, the men persecuted and dismissed by the Bourbons, become the opposition candidates of the restoration and the satisfied members of Louis Philippe's parliaments. Their opponents come into their own in 1848 and fill the parliaments of the republic. Finally, on the fall of the second empire, legitimists, Orleanists and republicans all emerge from their enforced retirement to dispute the spoils of power. The revolutions thus bring old men back into politics as well as introducing new men into it, and they are as much kaleidoscopes remixing old parties as generators of novel forces.[2]

How does the second empire fit into this pattern ? It is no gap in the history of France, as the republican historians assert. Like most governments issuing from revolution, it is based to a certain extent on new men, but it has strong ties with the régimes which preceded it. It thus represents an alliance of new and of old forces, and this book will seek to show its nature and its meaning.

[1] Quoted by S. Charlety, *La Restauration* (1911), 109.
[2] Cf. M.U. 1827, 1551.

CHAPTER II

How the foundations of a new Bonapartist party were laid

(1852)

AFTER the plebiscite had acclaimed his *coup d'état*, Napoleon, though apparently master of the nation, did not consider his task complete. He still needed allies for the government of the country. He did not believe that it was enough simply to have the peasants behind him. 'When one bears our name,' he wrote, 'and when one is at the head of the government, there are two things one must do : satisfy the interests of the most numerous classes and attach to oneself the upper classes.' [1] The politics of his period had two levels : that of the masses and that of the politicians. The people could provide a solid basis for his government but they could not govern themselves and they could only delegate their rights to him. Napoleon therefore needed men to help him : he had to form a new ruling class.

The way he did this can be seen in the parliamentary elections of 1852. He summoned a legislature to consist of 261 members, each representing a constituency of some 35,000 electors. All men over 21 could vote and stand. Napoleon, however, announced 'official candidates' and used all the resources of his prestige and his influence to urge the people to vote for them. Most of these candidates were successful and many of them were even elected unopposed. The election has therefore been regarded as a farce and the parliament which issued from it as a packed

[1] E. d'Hauterive, *Napoléon III et le prince Napoléon*, 58-9.

congress of loyal party men. A study of the correspondence in the government's files reveals, however, that this
view is erroneous and that the election was in fact highly
important. It was the provincial counterpart of the plebiscite and it effected great changes among the local rulers of
the country. It shows, too, how Napoleon did not seek to be a
mere dictator of the masses and how he did not call a parliament merely in order to fill it with puppets or nonentities.
'You will have noticed what is happening,' wrote Persigny
to Falloux. 'We, who have no friends except below, if we
wanted nothing but power, we would have done two
things: kept the salary for M.P.s and allowed the civil
servants to sit in parliament. We have done the opposite
and given the legislature to the upper classes. We have
openly supported and chosen our candidates, but from the
highest ranks of society, from the great landowners,
wealthy mayors and so on.' [1]

The minister of the Interior sent instructions in general
terms to the prefects and asked them to recommend men
to him who would be suitable as M.P.s, men who would
not only vote for the government but would bring real
strength to it, and whom he would nominate as its 'official
candidates' at the election. The prefects at once showed
that they had varying views as to what kind of men should
be chosen, and as to what the purpose of the election should
be. A few ardent ones wanted none but pure Bonapartists
in parliament and a clean sweep in the country. 'In
Haute-Garonne,' wrote Pietri, 'as in a great number of
other regions, the administration has until now left the
conduct of political affairs to the old parties. Instead of
putting itself in contact with the people, it placed itself
under the tutelage of the chiefs of these parties and thought
it had done a lot when it succeeded in grouping them

---

[1] G. Goyau, *Un Roman d'amitié* (1928), 160. M.P.s were paid under
the republic. Under the Orléans monarchy civil servants were allowed to
be M.P.s without having to give up their jobs.

around it under the name of *men of order*. No one, except perhaps M. de Maupas, had dared hoist the flag of Louis Napoleon here. This humble attitude of the administration fortified the influence of the old parties by discrediting the authorities and made any frankly Napoleonic candidature impossible.

'The elections of 1849, therefore, were simply the result of this situation . . . which the administration had so unfortunately accepted or created. Our business today is not to fall into the same mistake but to give the authorities sure and devoted auxiliaries. The *coup d'état* of 2 December has changed the situation but it has not been able to break the parties completely in which the elements of opposition will for long continue to exist. In my opinion, the legitimist party in particular will never rally honestly to Louis Napoleon. While submitting to him, it will seek to undermine him silently, fully ready to seize the most favourable moment to act against him openly. If this is so, the candidates to the legislature ought to be as far as possible men entirely devoted to the prince. I do not conceal from myself, *M. le Ministre*, the difficulties we shall perhaps encounter in securing the triumph of their candidatures in a department where the influence of M. de Remusat and the legitimist party has always been considered preponderant, but these difficulties do not appear to me to be insuperable.'[1]

Many prefects pointed out that the policy of seeking 'notables' presented political problems, since most notables had already taken part in politics and were for that reason undesirable. They were either hostile or they suffered from the unpopularity of their fallen régimes. The great landowners were, moreover, nearly all legitimists. One prefect said that his department had some men who were 'important through their social position, their fortunes, even their careers, as well as through the personal considera-

[1] F(1c) II 99, Haute-Garonne, prefect, 20.1.1852.

tion and legitimate influence which they enjoy and who therefore would also have had a right to seek the confidence of the people in every other situation except that in which we are today. But that is not the problem any more. If I have understood your meaning properly, *M. le Ministre*, my report must aim at indicating the men who by their outstanding services to the cause we serve and by their personal devotion to prince Louis Napoleon, who incarnates the needs and the wishes of the country, ought to be put forward for the favour of the electors. I must therefore first of all declare to you that to obtain the affection of the masses in my department it is necessary to be above all and exclusively Napoleonic: whoever in the present state of things, stands without fulfilling this condition will certainly fail even though he may have a great deal of public esteem and consideration. The problem is thus simplified. . . .'
So the prefect says and he proposes Maupas, the minister of Police, and Maupas' father and two generals — these men being the local Bonapartist celebrities.[1] In fact, of course, the problem had been made more difficult, for three of them, as public servants, were not eligible to stand. It was not as easy as that to find Napoleonic candidates.

The advice to destroy the power of the old gang came from other prefects too. 'The mission of the administration,' wrote one, 'which is a delicate and difficult mission, must be to form what I shall call the government party. Until now the administration has been under the thumb of the factions, now of one, now of the other. People have spent a lot of intelligence on this deplorable game but they have founded nothing. The time is favourable to recapture the high position which the government ought never to have lost: it must control the passions of the masses and not follow or elude them. . . . To enjoy the confidence of our rugged peasants, an energetic government is needed which proves to them that it knows how to punish and

[1] F(1c) II 98, Aube, prefect, 18.1.1852.

13

who are the perfects

how to protect.' [1]   Again and again the prefects repeat
that what is required is new men, free from ties to fallen
governments.[2]

Not all the prefects, however, were as brimful of energy
or as eager to create a new party of which they would be
the heads.   The weaker and more conciliatory among them
were easily impressed by the influence of the old parliamentary hands and believed them to be irremovable.   An
official of the ministry of the Interior complained indeed
that the new prefects 'are inclined in favour of candidates
who have previously been successful in elections and deny
too easily the chances of new men'.[3]   But these prefects
insisted that the government should choose popular men,
to avoid producing a reaction against it or provoking the
candidature of some popular local man.[4]   The prefect of
Bouches-du-Rhône, insisting that it was impossible to
ignore local conditions (which in his case of course meant
the strength of the legitimists), demanded that the official
candidates should be men 'who will represent best the
natural sympathies of the districts, while at the same time
giving the government the guarantees of sincere adhesion
and devotion which it has a right to demand'.[5]

This attitude degenerated among some prefects into a
simple desire to back the winner.   They discussed with
heat the 'chances' of the various candidates and as a result
some were chosen because 'they had the best chances' almost
irrespective of other considerations.[6]   There were, however, limits to what the government would tolerate in a
department where the prefect proclaimed himself helpless.

[1] F(1c) II 100, Haute-Loire, prefect, 14.1.1852.
[2] F(1c) II 98, Ardennes, prefect, 7.2.1852 ; 99, Haute-Garonne, undated note ; 99, Ille-et-Vilaine, prefect, 9.1.1852 ; 100, Lot, prefect,
14.1.1852 ; 102, Seine-Inf., prefect, 10.2.1852 ; 103, Var, prefect,
7.2.1852, etc.   [3] F(1c) III, Corrèze 7, note.
[4] F(1c) II 103, Var, prefect, 6.2.1852 ; 99, Ille-et-Vilaine, prefect,
19.1.1852 ; 102, Sèvres, prefect, 20.1.1852.
[5] F(1c) II 98, B.-du-Rhône, prefect, 27.1. and 5.2.1852.
[6] F(1c) II 101, H.-Marne, Persigny, 6.2.1852 ; 98, Aveyron, L. Jaoul to
Calvet-Rogniat, 27.1.1852.

It could not accept men who had been prominently hostile to it. 'However honourable the character of the candidates you propose may be,' wrote Persigny, 'it is impossible for the government to accept the former M.P.s who voted in favour of the quaestors' bill' in 1851, hostile to Louis Napoleon.[1] Men 'tarnished with the original sin of the protest of 2 December' were impossible unless they have good proof of conversion.[2] Persigny rejected one man because the prefect had forgotten his relations with Cavaignac, whose aide-de-camp he had been; and another for fear that he would inevitably fall under 'the influence of the salons of Paris'.[3] Objection was raised against others on the ground that they were related to leading politicians of the opposition.[4] There were thus many opinions as to what kind of candidate the government should support. One man, however, probably combined the most popular qualifications when he applied for the title of official candidate on these grounds: that he was the son of a prefect of the first empire, which made him 'Napoleonic'; that he was a new man, and therefore not a member of any Orleanist clique; that he had distinguished himself on 2 December, which meant he had rendered services to the cause and identified himself openly with it; that he was recommended by influential men, which put him in the right set and guaranteed his sincerity; and finally that he had good chances of winning.[5]

Now who was it who chose the official candidates and who thus recruited the party? There were in fact many influences at work. There is little evidence of any participation by Napoleon himself. It was he who chose the candidate for Corsica, where devoted candidates abounded and

---

[1] F(1c) II 99, Ille-et-Vilaine, 5.2.1852.
[2] F(1c) II 101, Oise, prefect, 3.2.1852, and 99, Eure-et-Loir, prefect, 11.1.1852.   [3] F(1c) II 100, Allier, Persigny, 21.1.1852.
[4] F(1c) II 102, Seine, letter of Leroy de St-Arnaud; 99, Eure-et-Loir, prefect, 20.1.1852; 102, Sèvres, prefect, telegram, 11.2.1852.
[5] F(1c) II 99, Hérault, note of 13.2.1852 by Brun.

where only his decision could put an end to their rivalries ; but there are only two other cases where he is actually known to have intervened.[1] In later elections the official candidates were generally approved by the council of ministers on the recommendation of the minister of the Interior, and the minister of the Interior is found 'taking the orders of the emperor' on whom he should recommend. Perhaps Napoleon was too busy with other things in 1852, perhaps he acted simply by word of mouth, but what is certain is that he did not draw up a list of 200 men to be packed into the parliament.

Curiously enough the minister of the Interior was not the man who made the parliament either. Persigny, it is true, set the tone of the election but he was less important in the choice of the official candidates. He was essentially the theorist of the election, the inspirer of the fight, the spirit behind the rousing of the masses and the denunciation of the enemy. His telegrams to his prefects, full of life and energy and sincerity, were as the stirring battle cry of a captain to his troops. 'Concern yourself only with the masses', he wrote. 'It is they who will make the election. Ask them resolutely to support men devoted to Napoleon.' 'I maintain that the action of the administration ought to be decisive in the forthcoming elections. If there is need, issue an energetic proclamation to support the friends and repulse the enemies of Louis Napoleon and the inhabitants of the countryside will answer your call.' 'Do not bother about [a certain opponent]. I am certain that the action of the administration will be decisive. Proclaim aloud the candidates of the government of Louis Napoleon. Appeal to the sentiments of the people. It is the masses who make elections today and not the old influences.'[2] A draft of a letter he wrote six months later for the local elections

---

[1] F(1c) III, Corsica 5, 6.2.1852 ; F(1c) II 98, Aube, 15.2.1852 ; 99, Eure-et-Loir, Persigny, 13.2.1852.

[2] F(1c) II 101, H.-Pyr. 13.2.1852 ; 99, Eure-et-Loir, 13.2.1852 ; 98, Charente, 13.2.1852, telegrams.

shows what the purpose behind all this was. 'It matters little', he wrote, 'that a few notorious enemies should be elected to the *conseil général*, what matters is that there should be no canton where the hand of the government has not at least sapped the foundations on which the old influences rested. . . . Overthrow the hold of the old influences on the minds of the people. . . . Do not fear to fight against the old parties . . . our business above all is to create a party.'[1]

Yet though his theory was full of fire, he showed a great deal of moderation in detail and was always ready to make concessions in departments where the opposition was strong. There is no evidence at all of his trying to cram the house with pure Bonapartists, and in fact he was extraordinarily cold to these men. The proposals he made were seldom orders. He would say to the prefect, 'Mr. X seems suitable, give me your opinion'; or 'Has he any chances?' He repeatedly gave proof of his willingness to compromise and to listen to advice. He had, it is true, his likes and his dislikes and he would not yield on everything. He was willing to accept, for example, a legitimist only 'if there is no Napoleonic candidature' in the constituency.[2] 'The government', he wrote, 'wishes to show moderation in its choices but not beyond a certain limit.'[3]

Here is a letter which illustrates his policy and at the same time shows his cordial relations with his prefects. 'My dear prefect . . . I am overwhelmed with the best information and after having weighed all the circumstances and consulted the government, here is what I think I must write to you. There are two names in your list which the government cannot accept, M. de Mepieu and M. de Faugier. The former is a respectable and moderate legitimist who I do not doubt must be rallied since you support

---

[1] F(1c) II 58, undated draft by Persigny, the above are alternative crossed-out phrases.　　　　[2] F(1c) II 100, Loire, 10.2.1852.

[3] F(1c) II 98, B.-du-Rhône, Persigny's telegram, crossed-out sentences, 13.2.1852.

him. But the same will happen to M. de Mepieu as has happened to so many others ; as soon as he gets to Paris he will be easily drawn in by the men of the salons who corrupt all who go near them. Besides, in a department such as yours, we must beware of the prejudice which prevails against members of the nobility and of the legitimist party. As for M. Faugier, he is not a reliable character : we know him and he would abandon us at the first opportunity.' Persigny went on to suggest that the prefect should do as Persigny advised, but that he should pretend that he was doing it on his own initiative, so as to keep intact his authority as prefect. He ended by expressing the hope that the prefect would shortly be promoted. What is more, the prefect in the end got his own way.[1]

If the masses were legitimist, Persigny was willing to make concessions, but they were so in only a few departments. 'There is at Montbrison', he wrote, 'a very respectable legitimist society which is not well placed to judge the opinions of the people. It would gladly see M. Maudre [made M.P.] but the people would not. M. Bouchetal-Laroche is a devoted man who will suit the sentiments of the masses better and you ought to be able to ensure his success.'[2] Persigny would thus hold firm when he thought the opposition leaders in a particular department were merely officers without an army. 'In the department of which you are in charge, the action of the government ought to be decisive . . . you ought to be able to ensure the success of your candidates.'[3] He was, moreover, no fire-eating advocate of force. On one occasion he was compelled to adopt an opposition candidate, a M. Lemaire, who had protested against the *coup d'état* : he made a virtue of the necessity and showed he could use such an opportunity to win over a former enemy. He got

[1] F(1c) II 100, Isère, Persigny's draft, 5.2.1852.
[2] F(1c) II 100, Loire, Persigny's telegram, 20.2.1852.
[3] F(1c) II 101, Cantal, Persigny's telegrams, 14. and 17.2.1852.

the prefect to convey the government's decision to the accompaniment of much flattery. 'I have carried out your instructions', wrote the prefect, 'with regard to M. Lemaire who is enchanted by the patronage which the government is giving him and by the good will you asked me to express to him in your name ; in return for which he expressed to me the great affection which he has for you personally.'[1]

It was not Napoleon, nor Persigny, but the prefects, who had the greatest single influence in choosing the official candidates. This is not surprising, for since the government had no intention of packing the parliament with a gang of former exiles, and since it meant the election to contribute to the overthrow of the provincial oligarchies, it needed knowledge of local conditions such as only the prefects possessed. The prefects were often well aware of this, and thus Haussmann, one of the most energetic of their number, demanded complete independence to do as he pleased. 'The position in which the prefects have been placed', he wrote, 'is as embarrassing as it is new. Formerly the government gave the candidatures time to appear and confined itself to choosing between them. The prefects even had almost complete freedom in this matter. Today, instead of waiting for the candidatures to appear and for the impression they make on the country to be capable of assessment, the government wants to assume both the initiative and the risks [of announcing its candidates itself]. Too much importance cannot therefore be given to weighing well the chances in this or that area, of each of the men who are to be elected. This task, for which the prefects are responsible, is made very difficult by the right you have reserved to yourself . . . to designate from Paris the candidates to be supported. This reserved right greatly hinders negotiations with possible candidates, since no serious person would think of risking giving an acceptance to an

---

[1] F(1c) II 101, Oise, prefect, 16.2.1852.

official who is not authorised in advance to promise him his support. It is besides painful for the head of a department to avow to anyone that the government does not leave the conduct of its politics to him.'[1] The government could not, of course, give the prefects a blank cheque as a matter of principle but in practice it was difficult, and indeed unwise, not to accept their proposals whenever possible.

Their strength can be seen, for example, in Pas-de-Calais. Here the government had insisted on a certain man being made official candidate. The prefect had objected to him in vain : the man was made official candidate, but the prefect nevertheless supported the man he had recommended, who was duly elected. It was the prefect who organised the elections on the spot and he would not do his job properly if he was not satisfied with the candidates he was supporting. It was the prefect, moreover, who supplied the bulk of the information on which the government based its decisions and, given a bit of energy and ability, he could therefore generally get his own way. One prefect thus sent very detailed information on the men he wanted made official candidates, with full and cogent reasons for his choice. Within a day Persigny replied: 'The government is willing to accept your list. I thank you for the precision and the clarity of the documents with which you supply me.'[2] Haussmann in Gironde likewise knew what he wanted, insisted on his proposals, and compelled the minister to yield.[3] Another prefect refused absolutely an influential candidate urged on him very strongly by Persigny on the ground that this man was not the son-in-law of a senator but merely the husband of a senator's adulterine daughter, and that the people would not vote for such a person.[4] Yet another whose proposals

[1] F(1c) III, Gironde 4, 7.2.1852.
[2] F(1c) III, Nord 6, 7. and 8.2.1852.
[3] F(1c) III, Gironde 4, 14.2.1852, Persigny.
[4] F(1c) II 102, Somme, prefect, 9.2.1852.

were rejected in Paris wrote to Napoleon : 'If I am not given complete liberty of action, I beg you, *Monseigneur*, to be good enough to transfer me and appoint me to another prefecture.' Persigny yielded and replied : 'I esteem your character and your devotion too highly to insist further. I therefore leave you free to act as you wish'. The prefect was all politeness ; he made concessions in turn and accepted one of Persigny's proposals. 'I have acted thus', he wrote, 'out of respect for the hierarchy. . . . I shall be very glad to find an opportunity to give you this proof of my regard.'[1]

In the difficult departments where the legitimists had powerful influence over the masses, the government did in fact give the prefects great independence almost from the outset. To Finistère, for example, Persigny wrote : 'In view of the difficulties you are experiencing, the government approves the candidatures of MM. de Mesonan and Conseil and leaves you entirely free to choose the others' ; and he made this note for the ministry : 'Give the prefect a blank cheque'.[2] The government thus showed that it agreed with the view of the prefect who wrote : 'I suppose that at Paris the political question dominates all others ; but when you are on the spot, when you live among the landowners of the region, when you feel local interests at every step, it is very difficult not to take them into account'.[3]

It was only the prefect who did not know his own mind who would be imposed upon by the government. There is a case in which Persigny wrote to a prefect : 'It is impossible to decide on such vague information as you give me. What do you propose for each constituency ?' A week later he gave up in despair. 'Since it is impossible to choose the candidates of the government on the basis of your reports, here are the ones who are adopted . . .'[4]

The result was that in almost half of the departments

[1] F(1c) II 100, Isère, 8. and 10.2.1852.
[2] F(1c) II 100, Loire-Inf., Persigny, 18.2.1852 ; 99, Ille-et-Vilaine, 20.2.1852 ; 99, Finistère, 15.2.1852.   [3] F(1c) II 98, Ain, 8.2.1852.
[4] F(1c) II 103, Var, 10. and 18.2.1852.

for which there is evidence, the prefects' suggestions were accepted. In the remainder, about half of their proposals were accepted. In all, therefore, at least two-thirds or three-quarters of the official candidates were proposed by the prefects. But this does not mean that they alone made proposals. The letters from generals, senators and influential patrons of every sort which poured into the ministry were quite as numerous as theirs. Many candidates thought they stood no chance unless backed by powerful friends, and yet their testimonials were seldom decisive. Baroche for example, got his candidate accepted in Seine-et-Oise, where he had built up influence, but many more of his recommendations were fruitless. It is noteworthy that Napoleon forwarded all the letters he received in favour of candidates to the ministry of the Interior without comment. Though unsolicited advice was, naturally enough, frequently ignored, Persigny did seek out the opinion of colleagues and men he trusted who could give him information about the departments from which they came. The prefects likewise consulted their sub-prefects, who in turn made inquiries of important mayors and notables, and a few even called meetings of them to choose the official candidate by vote.

The significance of this method which Napoleon adopted, of choosing his candidates through the administration, is that it meant a break with the practice of the republic and a disavowal of the Bonapartist party which had grown up in that period. The system had been to work through committees which had their heyday under the republic. In 1848 the Bonapartists had formed a committee like everybody else. Its headquarters were in the rue Montmartre, and Persigny and General Piat were its chiefs. Through their friends they appointed correspondents in the provinces, and they were active during the elections of December 1848 and April 1849. After the *coup d'état*, Morny, using the same system, had urged the prefects to establish Bonapartist committees in all arrondissements, cantons and communes, to ensure the success of the plebiscite by distributing ballot papers and propaganda. A central committee was formed in Paris at the ministry of Public Works, complete with statutes and with the title of 'National Electoral Association'. Marshal Exelmans, Grand Chancellor of the Legion of Honour, was its president; General Pelet was the chairman of the executive committee; and Napoléon de St-Albin, founder of the Society of 10 December in 1848, was one of its most active supporters. Early in 1852 this association issued a circular thanking and congratulating its helpers for their work in the plebiscite and appointing one man in each department to organise committees in all its subdivisions down to the commune. It is unlikely, however, that it found agents in anything like all the departments, for it obtained its recruits in a very haphazard way. Any man who wished to further the cause would, of his own accord, print a few thousand ballot papers and distribute them in his district. During parliamentary elections he would write to some great Bonapartist to ask whom he should support and he would in this way be brought into touch with the central organisation. Only rarely did it recruit more than scattered individuals, as happened when the Bretagne Insurance Company came forward and put its 300 agents at the association's disposal.

Now the association set about choosing its candidates for the election and it got busy collecting information in the established manner. The reports which poured in from its correspondents were put together by Gallix, a Paris journalist, and Roustain, deputy mayor of the Latin Quarter of Paris and deputy professor of law. Meanwhile its agents in the departments were active. General Rey, for example, 'Central President of all the Napoleonic committees of Isère since the month of November 1848', began to search for 'Napoleonic candidates known as such, serious men with public opinion on their side'. He had his plans all worked out. He intended to discuss the names he thought of with the prefect, and to add whoever the prefect suggested. He would then send his list with biographical details to the minister of the Interior for decision. The chosen candidates he would support in his Napoleonic newspaper, which he had founded in 1848 and which he had always kept independent of the administration. Great was his surprise therefore when suddenly 'from outside the Napoleonic supporters' candidates were chosen and announced by the prefect without consulting him — candidates whom he considered absurd and 'anti-Napoleonic'.[1] The committees found themselves the rivals of the prefects.

This rivalry was not essential. In Haute-Saône, the prefect had organised three election committees before the *coup d'état*, one for each arrondissement, in preparation for the legislative election which was to have been held in 1852. The organisation was elaborate and the aim precise. It was designed to support the revision of the republican constitution. It was headed by a 'committee of initiative', composed of local officials, councillors, professional men, officers of the national guard and leading landowners, all paying an entrance fee of 10 francs, or about 8 shillings. They would draw up a list of possible candidates, which they would submit to a larger meeting of representatives of the communes. They would choose the representative themselves but would include the mayors, priests and schoolmasters. The vote of this meeting would decide who the candidates would be. The men who attended it would then return to their villages to distribute ballot papers, posters and propaganda. This evidently is an excellent system of testing and influencing public opinion, and at the same time a system which the government could control.[2]

Yet the government from the start set out to destroy

---

[1] F(1c) II 100, Isère, Gen. Rey to minister of Interior, 31.1.1852.
[2] F(1c) II 103, Haute-Saône file.

these very committees which had done so much to help put it into power. 'Until now,' wrote Morny to the prefects, 'the custom in France has been to form electoral committees, and meetings of delegates. This system was very useful when men voted for a list. The system of voting for a list created such confusion and such a need to work together, that it was essential to act in committee. But today these sorts of meeting could have no advantage, since the election will be of single names. They would only have the inconvenience of creating premature ties, appearances of acquired rights which would only embarrass the people and deprive them of all liberty. Please dissuade the partisans of the government, therefore, from organising election committees.' [1]

Now why did Morny urge the abolition of committees whose formation he had ordered only a month before? [2] The main reason must have had a lot to do with the type of men who formed these committees. They were all essentially men of little standing, petty bourgeois, small-time politicians: a head caretaker of the Stock Exchange, a wholesale merchant, a postmaster, a carting contractor, notaries, barristers, retired soldiers. Now these men thought their time had come, their cause had triumphed, and they, its leaders, should get the spoils, the decorations, the jobs, the seats in parliament. But the government had made its policy clear, it wanted the support of the upper classes. It was embarrassed therefore, when, for example, Monavon put up his candidature, the leader of the Bonapartist committee in Latour du Pin, it is true — but a mere stripling, a notary's clerk who wrote poetry for the local paper. These committees gave such men ideas of 'acquired rights' which the government would not recognise: their reward could not come at the election, and they were disbanded.

[1] F(1a*) 2119, no. 107, 8.1.1852.
[2] Cf. F(1a*) 2110, no. 146, 10.12.1851.

The prefects, moreover, would not tolerate that the government should divide its favours and that there should be two channels of influence, one through the administration and one through the party. They wrote jealous (and amusing) rebukes to the committees to let them know their place. They complained to the government that it was 'strong enough by itself, and served sufficiently energetically by its prefects, to keep the initiative in and the conduct of the elections in its own hands'.[1]

The result of the dissolution of the party was that the influence of the smaller Bonapartist politicians on the choice of candidates was almost entirely removed. They could not refrain from continuing to send comments and advice; frequently written with difficulty in half literate hands on cheap paper; but the title 'recommended by the committee' ceased to carry weight. The secretary of the association himself, having failed to be adopted as the government's candidate in two different departments, stood as 'opposition Bonapartist candidate' against Baroche's Orleanist brother-in-law.

The official candidates were the government's candidates and were probably approved by the council of ministers. Persigny always talks of himself as being 'personally favourable' to a particular man and says that he only makes proposals to the government. But in practice his advice and that of the prefects was generally accepted.[2]

These were the makers of the parliamentarians of the second empire. It is a conclusion of considerable interest. It shows how the course of events was determined only slightly by the rulers in Paris, and to a much greater extent by the administrators in the provinces. It shows the importance of studying the subordinates as well as the leaders

---

[1] F(1c) II 101, Nièvre, 18.1.1852; 100, Isère, 8.1.1852; 103, Var, prefect to National Electoral Association, copy, 19.1.1852; F (1c)III, Calvados 6, prefect, 15.1.1852.

[2] F(1c) II 100, Maine-et-Loire. Persigny, 15.2.1852; 100, Haute-Loire, Romeuf, 6.2.1852; F(1c) III, Doubs 5, Persigny, 19.2.1852.

of the government. These men appear to be in the background to historians seeking the general trend of great events, but the people of the day saw far more of the subordinates, and to them it was the leaders who appeared to be in the background. Politics is thus brought to a more real level. The same will happen when it is seen not simply what the parliamentary constitution of the period was, but also who were the men who put it into practice.

Perfect,

Subordinates - people saw more of leaders - app in background

CHAPTER III

Where Napoleon found the recruits for his parliament

IN 1852 the party of the second empire had still to be formed. The elections of that year represent one stage in its formation, but so varied were the men in charge of it, so different their aims, so diverse the conditions in every part of the country, that the result was inevitably a heterogeneous collection and a motley alliance of men. Members of nearly all the parties were recruited into the fold.

The Bonapartists were the largest single group in the parliament, and yet they hardly formed a third of the total. First came the men who were Bonapartists by inheritance, whose names read like the roll of honour of the first empire. Three relations of Napoleon headed their ranks: Clary, Morny and Lafon de Cayx, nephew of King Murat. There were the sons of eight generals of the first empire and relations of five others.[1] There were sons of its ministers and prefects,[2] like Nougarède, grandson of Bigot de Préameneu who had helped to draft the Napoleonic code and son of a president of the imperial court of Paris, 'united by the marriage alliances of my family to all the families of the empire, owing all to the emperor . . .'[3] There were the sons of courtiers, chamberlains and judges.[4] There were seventeen who had served under the great Napoleon as

[1] Caulaincourt, Buquet, Caffarelli, Travot, Suchet, Lagrange, Hallez, Macdonald, Abbatucci. Dauzat-Dembarrère, Bourlon (nephew of Clauzel); Noualhier (son-in-law of Dulimbert, related to Jourdan and Senator Lemercier), Belliard (nephew of Lannes), Romeuf.
[2] Cambacérès, Champagny, Petiet, Lesperut; Prefects Beauverger, Ladoucette, Lepelletier, Plancy and Delamarre (nephew of Bignon).
[3] F(1c) II 98, Aveyron, his profession of faith.
[4] Duplan (whose mother served the empress), Chabrillan (son of a chamberlain), Duboys and Portalis (sons of judges). Miscellaneous: Beauvau, Lagrange, Viard.

prefects, soldiers or members of parliament.[1] There was a small group of men who were Bonapartists of the restoration and the July monarchy. Such were Belmontet, the poet of Bonapartism; Dr. Conneau, Louis Napoleon's physician in exile; Geiger, who had been brought up with Louis Napoleon, and who was the son of Prince Eugene's director general of domains; Mesonan, who had been at the Boulogne attempt.[2] Arnaud, a self-made merchant, the son of a labourer, filled with hatred of the old gang, was what might be called a radical Bonapartist, as also was Massabiau, who was as democratic as he was Bonapartist and for whom the workers voted on red ballot papers. Finally came the men converted only since the republic: members of Bonapartist committees at the presidential election, journalists and ministers who had supported the *coup*.[3]

Even these seventy Bonapartists were of very varied type. Few were 'pure Bonapartists', for, as the prefect of Cher wrote, 'Had I found an exceptional candidate, a politician, a Bonapartist of good old stock, who had come through the last thirty-five years without any contact with legitimism or Orleanism, I should have held out my hand to him and I should have said to you, Take him. But these men, of whom I have the honour to be one, are rare throughout the country and I think I can affirm that not a single one exists in the department of Cher.'[4] Beauverger, for example, son of a prefect of the first empire, was unsullied and proud of his 'life dedicated to the cult of memories'.[5] But the trouble was that it was almost impossible to be

[1] Houdetot, prefect; Thieullen, sub-prefect. Larabit, Normand, Lemercier, soldiers of the first empire; and also the following who later rose to be generals: Brunet-Denon (A.D.C. to Murat), Gorsse, Parchappe, Gellibert, Vast-Vimeux, Rogé, Duvivier, Mercier, M.P., baron of the empire.

[2] Cf. also Wattebled, Millet, Verclos and Didier.

[3] Kervéguen, Guyard-Delalain, Fouché-Lepelletier and Leroux. Noubel, Véron, Jubinal, Delamarre and Granier de Cassagnac, journalists. Delapalme (brother-in-law of Baroche), Maupas (father of the minister), Fortoul (brother of the minister of Education), Schneider, minister 1851, Chevreau (father of the prefect). Koenigswarter, and Bouchetal-Laroche (probably a friend of Persigny). [4] F(1c) III, Cher 4, 10.2.1852.

[5] F(1c) II 102, Seine-et-Marne, his circular.

both unsullied and a notable; for the unsullied withdrew into retirement and obscurity, obtained no favours and built up no influence. It was for this reason that the pure Bonapartists had great difficulty in getting seats, for, unless they were linked very closely with Napoleon personally, as, for example, Dr. Conneau was, the prefects objected that they were unknown and Persigny, thinking that they would consequently have 'poor chances', would not press for their adoption. The man who had the greatest difficulty in being adopted as official candidate, who had to move heaven and earth to succeed, was, oddly enough, Belmontet, who had devoted his life to the Bonapartist cause. He could not believe the opposition he encountered. 'No,' he wrote in despair, 'M. de Persigny will not do this injury to the old devotion of Belmontet! No, the head of the Napoleonic party will not dishonour the right of one of its first soldiers!'[1] Granier de Cassagnac, who was to become the staunchest of Bonapartists, only just got adopted in Gers after trying several other departments. In Calvados, a Bonapartist was adopted but then dropped in favour of an Orleanist, on the ground that his chances were poor. Thil and Napoléon de St-Albin of the Exelmans committee were rejected as were the Bonapartist newspaper editor in Hérault and the law professor of Caen, president of his town's '2 December committee'.[2] The trouble with them was that they were not notables, not polished, well-mannered men, as a prefect said, able to 'go into society'.[3]

Almost half of these Bonapartists were tainted with the favours of previous governments, and particularly that of Louis Philippe. Morny is the most famous of these, for though Louis Napoleón's half brother, he had been conservative M.P. under Guizot; but a more typical example of the species is Duboys. His father had been an officer and a judge during the first empire; an M.P. during the

---

[1] F(1c) II 102, Tarn-et-Garonne, 11.2.1852.
[2] F(1c) III, Calvados 6, 15.1.1852.
[3] F(1c) II 102, Somme, ministry note.

Hundred Days and then persecuted by the restoration: 'the memory of the emperor was a cult for him'. Duboys himself was a school-mate of Louis Philippe's son; in 1830 he was given a job in the magistracy and he rose to be advocate general of Angers. He was Bonapartist by birth, perhaps, but Orleanist by his generation.[1] Many Bonapartists became fully naturalised Orleanists in this way. Rambuteau's name, said a prefect, was linked with the empire, but rather more so with the monarchy of July. Persigny refused to accept as official candidate the son of Soult, marshal of the empire but also Louis Philippe's minister. The more recent memories were inevitably the strongest. A bare half of the Bonapartists were 'pure' and free from all other loyalties.

To whom, then, could the government turn to augment these slender ranks? Everybody's answer was, the new men, 'who have not been members of any previous parliament and who are consequently free and independent'.[2] Morny had urged that the government should scoop up the cream of self-made men who had recently risen to importance, who represented the youthful energy of the country, but who had not yet been corrupted by politics. Typical of these was Conseil, a merchant of Brest who, having made his own fortune, prepared to enter parliament on his own initiative. 'M. Conseil', wrote the prefect, 'is not an eminent man but is a wise and moderate man of sound judgment and perfectly recommendable in all respects. The government would be able to count on him.' He was accordingly adopted as official candidate,[3] as were some fifteen others, merchants, industrialists, lawyers of the same class as himself.[4] The new men were sometimes really non-political choices, as was, for example, a retired

[1] BB(6) II 134, his file.
[2] F(1c) II 98, Aveyron, Calvet-Rogniat's note on himself.
[3] F(1c) II 99, prefect of Finistère, 30.1.1852.
[4] Industrialists: Lefebure, Devinck, Descat, Quesné, Balay, Garnier, Charlier, Dugas. Merchants: Montané, Schyler, Fleury, Bois. Lawyers: David, Perret, Jollivet. Doctor: Girou.

forest commissioner described simply as a 'government man';[1] or an artist, son of a tailor, who had been sent to study art in Paris by his native town and who, now famous, a member of the Institute and officer of the Legion of Honour, was chosen to represent this town merely because he was the local celebrity.[2] Others, however, came from parliamentary families and were merely personally new men.[3] An example of the way such men joined the Bonapartist ranks is Bryas. His father and his uncle had been M.P.s; but he had married into another department into a family apparently related to Ducos, the minister of the Marine. Drawn by these new contacts, he 'burnt his boats with the old parties', founded a newspaper to support Napoleon, and came into parliament as a new man devoted to the cause.[4] In all there were about forty new men.

They were recruits. Allies were found in twenty-five members of the Orleanist opposition, of whom a dozen had been M.P.s. Many of the opponents of Louis Philippe had naturally come into their own in 1848: many of them were re-elected in 1848 and 1849 and thus, when the crisis of 1851 came, those who accepted Napoleon's solution to it were kept on to serve in the next parliament. They were the outs come in. In so far as the republic and the empire were a reaction and a fight against Orleanist influence, the opponents of Louis Philippe were Napoleon's obvious allies. Taillefer illustrates the evolution of these men well. He was the son of a regicide M.P. of the revolution. He was by birth the enemy of the Bourbons: the revolution of 1830 which was very left to start with, therefore brought him into the general council of his department. He inherited the leadership of the local radical opposition from his father, and in 1846 at length succeeded in being elected

---

[1] F(1c) II 102, Bas-Rhin, prefect, 6.2.1852.
[2] Lemaire of Valenciennes, Nord.
[3] Dalloz, 2 Duponts, Debelleyme, Etcheverry, Reinach.
[4] F(1c) II 99, Indre, 15.1.1852 and 10.2.1852. Others are Aymé, Riché, Godart, Louvet, Planté, Caruel, Gareau, Ledier, Veauce, De Voize, Marrast, Du Marais, Reveil.

to parliament. The revolution of 1848 destroyed his Orleanist opponents and raised him to the presidency of his general council. His wheel had come full circle. 'I am pure', he wrote, 'of all contact with the governments which have preceded your own. None gave me a favour, not even a ribbon for my buttonhole. I want to drop my political anchor, to make an end of it, and to make it with you.'[1]

Finally, there were about 70 men who were even more independent of the government: 35 of legitimist origin, 2 catholics, 18 conservatives (government men ready to serve under most régimes) and 17 Orleanists.[2] The classification of these men between the parties is sometimes difficult and arbitrary, but they were in any case very independent allies whom the government accepted not from choice and not from the supposed desire to create a 'party of order', but from necessity and from policy. It had no love for Orleanists, and Persigny complained of a man, prefect throughout the reign of Louis Philippe, as being 'an incorrigible Orleanist'.[3] Five of them were accepted after hesitation and resistance on Persigny's part. Another four came from Pas-de-Calais: they were M.P.s in 1851 and

[1] F(1c) III, Dordogne 5, Taillefer, 20.1.1852. Chasseloup, Lemercier, Bidault, Billault, Delthiel, Le Gorrec, Choque, Desjobert, Delavau, Debretonne, Sallandrouze. Eschasseriaux, Lemercier son, Ste-Hermine, Parieu, Mouchy, Soullié, Gisclard, Clermont-Tonnerre, Lanquetin, Levavasseur, Bertrand, Faugier, Ouvrard. Three opponents of the restoration, Bavoux, Lecomte, F. Favre.

[2] Legitimists : Jouvenel, Andelarre, Bourcier, Ravinel, Partouneaux, Rochemure, La Guéronnière, Wendel, Torcy, Durfort de Civrac, Bûcher de Chauvigné, O'Quin, Barbentane, Gouy, Carayon, Chauvin-Lenardière, Lormet, Jonage, Rigaud, Remacle, Curnier, Uzès, Calvière, Haichois, Mortemart, Flavigny, Mepieu, Argent, Tromelin, Parmentier, Duclos, Pongérard, Roques, Arjuzon, Chazelles.
  R.C.s : Montalembert and La Tour.
  Conservatives : Demesmay, Grammont, Lelut, Boissy, Lemaire, Durand, Renouard de Bussière, Migeon, David of Sèvres, Janvier, Fortoul, Seydoux, Clebsattel, Lacave, Talhouet, Chanterac, Tixier.
  Orleanists : Vautier, Leroy-Beaulieu, Monier, Renouard, Chauchard, Herlincourt, Lequien, Hérambault, Lefebure, Hermant, Randoing, Bigrel, Tauriac, Mercier, Gouin, Roulleaux-Dugage, Bertin (I.-&-V., defeated), Du Miral.

[3] F(1c) II 99, Hérault, Roulleaux-Dugage to Michel Chevalier, 13.2.1852.

the conservative prefects thought their re-election inevitable. Some of these men, and some of the conservatives, had co-operated in the movement for the revision of the constitution, but most were merely accepted by tame prefects. In the eastern Pyrenees Durand, the department's leading landowner, was adopted because he had long opposed the domination there of the republican Arago family. Now that the Aragos were defeated, it was his turn to represent the department in parliament. Another man, who had been M.P. for fifteen years, was supported by all parties because of his 'good will and devotion to the inhabitants'.[1]

What is most interesting, however, is the government's policy towards the legitimists. All sorts of circumstances favoured their entering the parliament. The law giving M.P.s no salary and excluding civil servants from their number restricted membership to rich men. Morny's circular demanded the election of great landowners, Persigny's said that their political antecedents should be ignored. The list of politicians expelled after the *coup d'état* included no legitimists; a decree of 22 January 1852 confiscated the property of the Orléans family. All this pointed in the same direction. The prefects wrote to the ministry in puzzlement that nearly all the great landowners were legitimists. 'It is to be feared', wrote Haussmann, 'that membership of parliament will be the privilege of the great landowners and that the legitimist opinion will come out in great strength. Its partisans do not conceal that they do in fact count a lot on this result. It will be, moreover, the first time that we have seen the systems of unpaid M.P.s and of the exclusion of officials applied at the same time.'[2] The prefect of Finistère was equally puzzled. 'The government', he wrote, 'is evidently dealing carefully [*ménager*] with the legitimists. . . . What ought my conduct to be?

[1] F(1c) II 102, Tarn-et-Garonne, Janvier.
[2] F(1c) III, Gironde 4, 15.1.1852.

Can I launch a frontal attack on the opponents ? . . .
Ought I, on the contrary, to seek to appease, to conciliate,
to convert the recalcitrants ?' [1]

The reasons for this attitude to the legitimists can only
be guessed at. Did Napoleon fear their strength, for they,
unlike the Orleanists, had great influence on the masses ?
Were they natural allies against the Orleanist, was it an
inheritance of common opposition to Louis Philippe ?
Persigny was the friend of Falloux and there is a draft in
his hand saying : 'The government, at my request, decided
not to oppose M. Bûcher de Chauvigné [a legitimist], the
friend of M. de Falloux', who was duly made official candidate.[2] Did he have a general sympathy for them ?
Probably the government acted in this way not from
policy but simply at the dictate of circumstance. The
legitimists included uncompromising ultras but also
moderate men whose legitimism had become theoretical,
hereditary, a mark of good breeding, like the membership
of an exclusive club. There was hope of rallying them.
They had been out of office and deprived of influence long
enough to begin to despair. The marquis de Beausset-
Roquefort, M.P. before 1830, said that he would be eter-
nally grateful to the minister if he would do him the very
great service of adopting him as official candidate, 'because
it would enable me to re-enter the political career in a
decent manner. . . . You know me well enough to be able
to affirm that . . . my co-operation will be honest, without any mental reservations, and my fidelity as complete
as that of the most devoted friends of the government. It
is not of the men who remained loyal in 1830 that distrust is
possible.'[3] Some of these legitimists had already 'rallied'
when they were adopted by the government ; some com-
mitted themselves to support it when they accepted its

[1] F(1c) II 99, Finistère, 19.1.1852.
[2] F(1c) II 100, Maine-et-Loire, 15.3.1852.
[3] F(1c) II 98, Bouches-du-Rhône, 5.2.1852, to minister of Interior.

patronage; the rest, it was hoped, would 'rally' in the future.

Their varied attitudes can be seen in two examples. 'Though I am a legitimist by principle,' wrote another marquis, 'I have never adopted the Policy of the Party. I did not emigrate into the provinces in the first years of the Monarchy of July, nor later contract those monstrous alliances which overthrew it. As a Government Man and a Man of Conciliation, I moved towards the Conservative Party which carried me into Parliament [in 1846]. . . . In a spirit of conservatism and in the interests of the country, I loyally supported the De Facto Government, which had none of my personal sympathies. . . .'[1] Another type can be seen in a farmer, who 'is not a man of the salon — he is a country gentleman who wants the decoration I asked for him. You will do anything you please with him. He will vote for the government without saying a word.'[2]

The legitimists were, however, not sought out: it was merely that the prefects thought them the best candidates, and this accounts for about half of them. Flavigny, for example, was believed to be irremovable. 'His superior position, the immense consideration he enjoys, and the just influence he has won by the innumerable services which for the past twenty years he has not ceased to render to the district and to people,' appeared to make his choice inevitable.[3] The other half of the legitimists represented departments where their party was considered so powerful that the government decided to support moderate members of it in order to avoid openly hostile ultras. The prefects insisted that some compromise with them was essential. 'The numerical strength of the legitimist party', wrote one, 'does not allow me to doubt that it would be master of the election in the department of Hérault if it decides to unite

[1] F(1c) II 101, Orne, letter from Villedieu de Torcy to sub-prefect, 26.1.1852, and copy of another in prefect's letter of 3.3.1852.

[2] F(1c) II 100, Isère, prefect, 7.2.1852.

[3] F(1c) II 99, Indre-et-Loire, Quinemont's letter.

for the purpose. . . . I regard it a duty imposed on me both by gratitude and by wise policy, to contain with tact but with firmness this formidable party, always ready to accept . . . jobs which give influence, in order to make them serve the success of their personal views and their eternal hopes of the future. I had therefore to get down to seeking candidatures which were not the expression of the legitimist opinion, but which at the same time would not be sufficiently hostile to it to be the signal for a fight in which their numbers would defeat us.'[1] Michel Chevalier, who was influential in Hérault, told Persigny, 'The legitimists are too strong in the department for us not to give them their share, and of all their men the best for the president is M. . . .'[2] A few prefects even suggested abstaining from putting up an official candidate rather than suffer certain defeat.

There was of course resistance to this policy of yielding. Ought not the government to have a candidate 'of its choice, chosen by it and recognised as such, so as to counterbalance the legitimist influence?'[3] In one department the prefect had urged this policy of yielding. Fortoul, the minister of Education, protested. 'If you want legitimists to represent Bouches-du-Rhône, you have only to follow the advice of M. de Suleau [the prefect]. But if you choose M. Guien [whom Fortoul preferred, an Orleanist it appears, who was not in fact adopted] and if he accepts, you will create a great . . . governmental influence in a part of the country which has too long been abandoned.' The prefect, however, claimed that 'the most certain method of dissolving the old parties in this department is to borrow their leaders whenever they frankly accept the new order of things, and the number as well as the opportunity of these borrowings must be determined, it seems to me, by the real strength of the local influences which we wish to win

[1] F(1c) II 99, Hérault, prefect, 20. and 26.1.1852.
[2] *Ibid.*, pencil note by Persigny of a conversation with Chevalier.
[3] *Ibid.*, note by Huc.

over'.[1] On the other hand, in certain parts of the country the legitimists were unpopular and the nobles disliked. The government compromised. In only one case, that of Gard, did it deliver up the department entirely to the legitimists, but here there were special circumstances. Persigny regretted his decision as soon as he had made it and attributed it to incorrect information. Usually the legitimists were given a third or half of the seats in their strongholds. One seat in Vaucluse, for example, was given to a Bonapartist, 'which would be an advance on the road of Napoleonic principles', but the second was given to a legitimist 'to conciliate a considerable party and to obtain the even more considerable support of the clergy'.[2]

When the government in this way chose men openly calling themselves legitimists, was it impotently admitting enemies into its parliament? Sometimes it was and sometimes it was not. It had two ways of winning a hold on such enemies: the system of official candidates and the professions of faith. When a man publicly accepted the patronage of the government, he became a declared collaborator if not an actual convert. He owed the government something in return for its patronage. As a legitimist said, 'It is a question of honour . . . for me to support whether I like it or not, a government whose support and help I solicit'.[3] Another declared that a legitimist who accepted the title of official candidate 'would appear to me to lose his dignity and his independence', and he agreed to accept it himself only if the government allowed him to write to the leaders of his party to assure them that his independence was inviolate.[4]

A man who accepted the patronage of the government separated himself from his old party, but did not therefore

[1] F(1c) II 98, Bouches-du-Rhône, note by Fortoul, and prefect, 10.2.1852.   [2] F(1c) II 103, Vaucluse, prefect, 15.1.1852.
[3] F(1c) II 98, Ardèche, sub-prefect Largentière to Chevreau jnr., 7.2.1852.
[4] F(1c) III, Gard 5, Calvière to minister of Interior, 23.2.1852.

become a slave of the government. Persigny did not demand promises of obedience but simply that 'the candidates should in their circulars express themselves clearly in favour of the new order of things'.[1] This circular might take such a form as this: 'I am firmly convinced that to desert the cause of Louis Napoleon in the present or in the future would be to desert the cause of France and of civilisation. In a word I make profession of devotion, of loyalty, of respect and of sympathy, absolutely and without mental reservations, for the prince and for his government.' The author of this declaration was a legitimist, to one of whose children the comte de Chambord had stood godfather.[2] The aim was not to make such men puppets but to compel them to burn their boats and to ostracise themselves from their former party. They would thus be forced to stay on Napoleon's side since they were traitors to their old friends.

These then were the official candidates, but their mere choice did not ensure their election. Many people seemed to think, it is true, that a seat in parliament was a job in the government's gift, but it should by now be clear that the government did not consider its task to be so simple. The election of 1852 was, in fact, a serious affair. The smallness of the vote in favour of the government is not realised. There were

> 9,809,824 electors
> 6,223,582 voted
> 5,195,178 for government candidates
> 820,745 for opposition candidates
> 131,765 for miscellaneous candidates
> 75,894 votes were blank or annulled.[3]

[1] F(1c) II 100, Marne, Persigny, 7.2.1852; 102, Somme, Persigny, 10.2.1852.

[2] F(1c) II 102, Saône-et-Loire, Barbentane.

[3] F(1c) II 58. The figures of the opposition and the miscellaneous men given here are corrected ones. The clerk in this document put the figures of Vienne in the wrong column.

Thus, though the government may have got 83 per cent of the votes cast, only 53 per cent of the electorate voted for it and it therefore got a bare majority. The total of opposition candidates elected was small : 4 republicans and 2 legitimists. Only 5 official candidates had to undergo a second ballot because they did not get the votes of a quarter of the electorate. But within their constituencies government candidates were, in addition, defeated in whole districts.[1] Moreover, in twenty-six departments, that is in a third of the country, the government candidates were returned by a minority of the electorate. The opposition figures do not sound impressive but in fact they were not spread out evenly over France. There was no serious contest in two-fifths of the constituencies, there was some contest in another two-fifths, but the strong opposition was concentrated in the remaining fifth where over half (57 per cent) of the opposition votes were cast. In these latter constituencies, the opposition obtained 471,000 votes against the government's 835,000 ; and it is all the more remarkable because these constituencies are concentrated in clearly marked areas — the west, the north and the south-east.[2]

The abstention varied enormously in different regions, and it was particularly overwhelming in the towns. For France as a whole the figure is 37 per cent but in Cette (Hérault) 77 per cent abstained, and the official candidate was voted for by 12 per cent of the electorate. Some large towns voted no differently from the countryside (*e.g.* Lille, Arras, Clermont-Ferrand, Lyons, Auxerre, Rouen, Napoléon-Vendée) but two-thirds abstained in Strasbourg, Sedan, Lisieux, Amiens, Bourg (Ain), La Rochelle and Aix ; 54 per cent in Marseilles, 75 per cent in St-Étienne,

[1] Towns : Brest, St-Étienne, Marseilles, Béziers (Hérault), Crest (Drôme), Beaune (Côte-d'Or), Elbeuf (Seine-Inf.), Auxerre (Yonne). In one-third of the communes of Loire-Inf. (3) ; in three of the cantons of Aveyron (2) ; in two of Corrèze (2) ; in one arrondissement of Creuse (1). C. 1336-9.   [2] See the map on p. 172.

81 per cent in Vierzon (Cher). The contrast between town and country can be seen, for example, in Gironde. In the constituency of Bordeaux intra-muros 70 per cent abstained ; in Bordeaux extra-muros 53 per cent abstained ; in the three rural constituencies only 42, 43 and 46 per cent did.[1] This abstention of the towns had a definite political significance. In the election of 1849, the abstention was roughly the same in total, 33 per cent, but it was greatest in the country and least in the towns.[2] The elections show that, though all the nation may have voted in favour of Napoleon at the plebiscite, it was very divided when it had to descend from general principles to local details.

The opposition was certainly not silent. It faced innumerable obstacles : its leaders had been persecuted, its newspapers suppressed, its printers and its canvassers obstructed. Yet not a few managed to tour their constituencies and distribute their propaganda, to 'move heaven and earth to succeed'.[3] *The Times*, which was no friend to Napoleon, reported that in the capital at least 'no impediment was placed in the way of any party' ; in some constituencies every poster of an official candidate had one of its opponent's beside it and in others there were no posters but instead very active agents distributing ballot papers.[4]

Who then were the 250 opposition candidates ? The smallest number among them were Orleanists, and those Orleanists who did stand were generally not very hostile to the government. The way they thought can be illustrated by this story. In the department of Ain, Morny had accepted an Orleanist but Persigny had later rejected him. The man whom the government chose, a legitimist called Lormet, ignored the Orleanist gentlemen who had been used to managing elections, and left the propaganda entirely

---

[1] F(1c) III, Gironde 4.
[2] G. Genique, *L'Élection de l'Assemblée Législative en 1849* (Paris, 1921), 32.
[3] F(1c) III, Corrèze 7, 22.2.1852 ; F(1c) II 98, Côtes-du-Nord, 18.2.1852.   [4] *The Times*, 1. and 3.3.1852.

to the prefect. The local judge went to see the prefect and told him that the notables, 'society', had had a meeting, that they were 'profoundly hurt by the attitude of M. de Lormet towards them, they regarded it a duty to protest against a candidature which was put up as a defiance; and that they had just got M. de Courcelles [a former Orleanist M.P.] to stand. . . . We cannot withdraw; it is a duty which is imposed on us by our regard for our dignity before the eyes of the population of the town of Bourg. . . .'[1] These men were simply furious that their old control of local politics was being challenged. Most of the Orleanists, however, abstained for the same reason that they abstained in 1848: they were stung by the *coup* as they had been by the fall of their monarchy: they were overawed and struck numb by the astounding result of the plebiscite.

The 'reds' also largely abstained; and together with the Orleanists they probably account for the great abstention in the towns. They had, however, more candidates than the Orleanists, and theirs were openly hostile. What is remarkable about them is the way they got large votes from little effort. They won a seat in Lyons despite the arrest of their leaders, despite their having no election committees or even newspapers in which to announce their candidatures. In Marseilles the republican candidate obtained 5000 votes even though he had put himself up only two days before the election. Their method generally was to pass the word round among their friends at the last moment, that they would vote for some great republican in exile or some locally well-known leader. In this way they obtained considerable votes for absent candidates. Sometimes they gave their votes to an opposition candidate of another party. The government was much impressed by their discipline.[2]

[1] F(1c) II 98, Ain, prefect, 22.2.1852.
[2] BB(30) 403, *procureur général*, Grenoble, 18. and 26.2.1852, 9.3.1852. F(1c) III, Nord 6, prefect, 16.3.1852. F(1c) III, Meurthe 6, prefect, 6.3.1852.

There was some opposition which merely represented personal or local rivalry. One opponent was a popular solicitor who had headed the poll in 1848 and 1849 and who was simply a 'good chap' without political significance. Another stood because the official candidate was a stranger to the district. A third was a man with 'a numerous clientèle of men to whom he has rendered services and who, without bothering too much about his political opinions, go about proclaiming everywhere his obligingness and the readiness with which he places his credit at the disposal of everyone'.[1] In Dijon the mayor was the official candidate; his opponent was the deputy mayor who had just been dismissed after a quarrel. The mayor of Crest was so proud of the decoration he had received for his conduct on 2 December that 'he felt himself obliged to stand'.[2] The legitimist who was elected in Maine-et-Loire owed a great deal to the fact that his constituency consisted of two arrondissements; he came from one of them, and the official candidate from the other. Their struggle was thus to a considerable extent a matter of local rivalry. The victor was a young man of an old local family, who had always lived in his country house and devoted himself to local improvements, social welfare and religious institutions. On his election he hastened to inform the prefect that he had no intention of becoming 'an opposition man'.[3]

The strongest opposition came from the legitimists. As in the reign of Louis Philippe, their official policy was abstention, in order to prevent the party from collaborating and so disintegrating. Many, however, refused to allow their influence to rust from disuse and to abandon the gains made since 1848. The editor of the legitimist newspaper in Finistère told the prefect that his party would do all it could to overthrow Louis Napoleon and that it hoped to

---

[1] Bochard in Ain, Auliac in Cantal; F(1c) II 99, Indre, prefect, 18.2.1852.
[2] F(1c) III, Drôme 5, prefect, 13.2.1852.
[3] F(1c) II 100, Maine-et-Loire, prefect, 4. and 30.3.1852.

succeed.[1] Their activity became intense: meetings were held, candidates chosen. Then suddenly in many parts of the country they fell silent. Their candidatures were withdrawn. They may have received some threat from their king, or they may have been unable to agree on whom to put up. Even so, despite these withdrawals, their opposition was powerful. They had candidates in all the constituencies of three western departments and all together they put up about thirty-five important candidates, mainly in the west and south.

It is a stock belief that the second empire was established with the co-operation of the church. However, whatever the policy at Paris may have been, in the provinces the clergy were frequently hostile. The bishops opposed the official candidates in at least four departments of the west and even circulated orders in favour of the legitimists, which their clergy read out from their pulpits. Where a candidate was anti-clerical or unpleasing to the church for any reason, the clergy did not hesitate to oppose him, as happened in seven departments.[2] In Moselle and Ardèche they lent their aid against the protestant official candidates. Very often, of course, the church did support the government, but it was no obedient instrument and a very uncertain ally from the beginning.

The elections of 1852 show what the second empire meant. It did not represent a mere dictatorship of the masses, but sought to combine aristocracy with democracy and to build society in the shape of a pyramid, with the people as its base and a hierarchy of merit at its top. The driving force within it was ambition and worldly honour open to all was its reward. It enabled the peasants to vote for the left — for the revolutionary who had defied the

---

[1] F(1c) II 99, Finistère, prefect, 12.2.1852.

[2] Prefects' reports F(1c) II 99, Finistère, 12.2.1852; 100, Loire-Inf., 28.2.1852; 103, Vendée, 25.2.1852; 99, I.-&-V., 25.2.1852; 98, H.-Alpes, 28.2.1852; 98, C.-du-N., 13.3.1852; 101, Cantal, 21.2.1852; 102, Somme, 27.2.1852; 102, Sèvres, 3.3.1852; P.-de-C.; Aveyron; cf. 103, H.-Vienne, 23.2.1852.

constitution and against the old gangs and the nobles —
but at the same time to vote for the right, for order, for
property, for the family and for religion.

The elections show, too, how the seed of the liberal
empire was within it from the start. Its supporters included notables capable of participation in power, many of
whom had already tasted the pleasures of parliamentary
government under the monarchy of July. The demand
for the liberal empire from within the parliament is therefore to be expected. That from outside it is to be expected
no less. The old parties did not acclaim it and it was only
a question of time before they reawoke from their stupor.
The towns it never conquered, and they remained latent
enemies within it. The opposition of the end of the reign
was no less the revival of long-silent foes than the dissatis-
faction of a new generation. Its early years are no less
interesting or important than the violent struggles amid
which it ended.

CHAPTER IV

What politics meant to the members of parliament

NAPOLEON is asserted to have said, 'The empress is legitimist, my cousin is republican, Morny is Orleanist, I am a
socialist; the only Bonapartist is Persigny and he is mad'.
If such was the division among the leaders of the empire,
would it not be at least equal among its followers who, it
has been seen, were recruited from equally varied sources ?
Did the empire then represent no definite creed, and was it
merely a jumble of ideals and prejudices brought together
by accident and doomed to disintegrate at the first shock
of failure ? It has become a habitual pastime for historians
of this period to dissect Napoleon, to show up the divers-
ity of his background and the contradiction of his aims, and
thus to conclude that he was bound to fail. Yet his motley
qualities were perhaps necessary for a man engaged in
transforming a country in which the old and the new stood
confronted and unreconciled; and he was, moreover, by
no means unique in his age. Disraeli was in many ways his
counterpart in England, pursuing a similar task, and bizarre
and mystical like him. Their followers were equally
divided in both countries and they both had to deal with
all extremes from the most progressive radicalism to the
highest toryism.

Now the parliamentarians of the second empire represented many different shades of opinion but the remarkable
fact is that there were very few supporters of absolutism
amongst them. The extreme right was led by Baron
Jerome David, said to be the illegitimate son of King Jerome
Bonaparte and in any case certainly his godson and a great

confidant of the empress. With his military moustache and stern features suggestive of a Prussian Junker, he looked the part of a high reactionary. He spoke seldom and poorly, and his election as vice-president of the house represented simply an acknowledgement of the strength he derived from his back-stairs influence and from the vigour of his convictions. The views of his party were expressed by one of his followers. They were 'conservatives', he said. They believed that politics was not a matter for the people. The electors had no business with cabinet secrets; nor ought they to waste their time listening to inexperienced young men explaining great issues to them instead of getting on with useful work. Their task was to elect decent people to parliament and to give them a free hand to decide the affairs of the state. They did not deny that France loved liberty; but by liberty they understood merely equality before the law.[1] Yet even this group did not deny the theoretical merits of the need for reform and concessions; they objected only that progress was impossible without order in the streets and they counselled not resistance to all change, but merely procrastination.[2]

Many of the retired soldiers in parliament were likewise stalwart upholders of 'order' but with a more positive policy of using it to obtain glory. 'What France wanted above all was to resume the place in the world which its genius merited and which its valiant legions would know how to defend.' The empire for them represented the antithesis of the reign of Louis Philippe, with its fear of risks and of action; it represented the concentration of forces in a great patriotic movement for material and political glory.[3]

The bulk of the conservatives, however, were rather the

[1] Baron de Benoist, ACL 1868, 4. 166-9.
[2] Jerome David, CRCL 1860, 264; ACL 1861, 1. 231-7; ACL 1866, 3. 163-8; ACL 1869, 2. 49-59.
[3] Marquis de Nesle, ACL 1862, 2. 96-7; ACL 1863, 1. 97-8.

spiritual descendants of the provincial nobility of the eighteenth century. There were some among them, it is true, who had the Orleanist disinclination for 'great things', which were expensive, and preferred 'great speeches', parliamentary government, which cost nothing and increased their own importance. There is no doubt that the patriotic urge to lead the world appealed to most of them, and for this they were glad to have a Napoleon at the head of the state. But they had no use for the social consequences of Bonapartism. Du Miral, a provincial advocate general till the revolution of 1848 forced him into agriculture, later a vice-president of the house and a leader of another nuance of conservatism, rose in anger to deny that the empire had anything to do with democracy. He denounced the doctrine of the rule of the greatest number. 'The present empire', he repeated, 'is not democracy incarnate, it is not the republican idea crowned : it is monarchy . . . it is a real monarchy.'[1] What these men wanted was a combination of monarchy with aristocracy, which meant decentralisation, self-rule in local affairs, and the central government confined to the conduct of such matters as foreign policy. Liberty required 'the counterweight of an aristocratic or monarchic government'.[2] The government must therefore not seek to destroy the aristocracy but ought to strengthen it. 'When a proper government uses the power which it has at its disposal to destroy an ancient, useful, honourable and consequently a legitimate influence, it is not strengthening the principle of authority, it is only weakening the moral force of society and strengthening the revolution which can only gain ground when the barriers which hold it back are lowered.'[3] It was impossible, they claimed, to govern a country without an aristocracy. 'What can you expect to happen to a

---

[1] CRCL 1856, 528 ; CRCL 1860, 517.
[2] André de La Charente, ACL 1864, 2. 336-8.
[3] Baron de Jouvenel, ACL 1863, 3. 179-80.

democracy of 38 million souls, increasingly levelled out each day by social and political equality, without an aristocracy and so without guides, abandoned every morning to the perils of the press which poisons it and leads it astray, without religion, greedy of pleasure, seeking by methods right or wrong the gold which provides this pleasure; therefore, having very little time to give to the forum and to public affairs, and yet called upon to govern itself and all alone! In truth this phenomenon has no precedent in any time or among any people. [As I said in 1858] . . . France with its universal suffrage, which levels the people out [*qui en fait une poussière du peuple*], seems to me to be destined to fall incessantly from despotism into anarchy and from anarchy into despotism.'[1] In practical terms, their ideal meant the rule of the provinces by the notables, by *conseils généraux* to be turned into new provincial estates. To the more reactionary, this would be a means of holding the masses in check: to the liberals it was a way of educating them for self-government, by giving them practice on a local scale.[2]

This paradise of country gentlemen was very far from the ideal of the 'democratic' Bonapartists. For them the second empire was the régime of self-made men, and they claimed that its true character was shown by Napoleon's calling himself a *parvenu*.[3] It represented above all the principle of equality, 'dear to all men risen from the ranks of the people'.[4] 'It has on its side universal suffrage and a glorious *parvenu* represents admirably all those who want to *parvenir*, that is to say, democracy.'[5] The nobility had been dethroned in 1830, the bourgeoisie in 1848, all that remains today is the people and at its head, the emperor of a 'crowned democracy'.[6] 'The best characteristic of the

[1] Louvet to Ollivier, 26.10.1871, Ollivier papers.
[2] Pinard, ACL 1870, 2. 355-8. Chasseloup-Laubat's project for local councils, 1871, in his papers. [3] Taillefer, CRCL 1858, 514-15.
[4] Laroche-Joubert, ACL 1870, 5. 374.
[5] Taillefer, M.U. 1853, 554. [6] Piré, CRCL 1859, 196-7.

imperial government is to have delivered public affairs from the hands of minorities and newspapers into those of everybody . . .' and the essential thing about the régime was that 'it was the government of all substituted for the government of a few'. Its merit was that it knew how to make democracy work and how to prevent it from lapsing into demagogy. It sought to render the masses conservative by giving them something to conserve, and by occupying itself perpetually in improving their lot.[1]

It was this last aspect of the empire which appealed to the St Simonians in parliament. Heirs of another type of the eighteenth century, the reformers who saw in the king the only power strong enough to fulfil their aims, they found their ideal in this régime, directed by one man, but concerned with the well-being of the whole nation. They rejoiced in its gifts of cheap food, railways, roads, and canals, the essentials of rapid economic progress; they acclaimed it for bringing prosperity without precedent, social legislation, the welfare state, the raising of France to the first rank among the economic powers.[2]

'Napoleon represented for me, as a native of Ardennes, the protest against 1815; for me, as a landowner, as an industrialist, as a lawyer who knows the peasants and the people thoroughly, Napoleon was at once the guarantee of order and the promise of assistance within the limits of possibility.'[3]

Yet even these Caesarian democrats did not believe that Napoleon should rule by himself, and, as time passed, most of them demanded that they should have a share in his power and that parliament should be associated with him. If they did not go to the extent of demanding parliamentary government, they insisted on the government of the country with 'the co-operation and with the advice of

[1] Granier de Cassagnac, CRCL 1860, 503 and 1148-50.
[2] Nogent St-Laurens, CRCL 1854, 64-7; Koenigswarter, CRCL 1856, 32-4.
[3] F(1c) II 98, Ardennes, Riché-Tirman to minister of Interior, 26.1.1852.

the country'.[1]   Nearly all types in the legislature were
therefore opposed to the indefinite maintenance of the
constitution of 1852.

It would be an oversimplification, however, to suggest
that the new self-made men were in favour of Caesarian
democracy and that the heirs of great names or fortunes
were in favour of decentralisation.   It is in any case impossible to discover the real opinions of the great mass of silent
back-benchers.   These men must be approached from
another angle.   The reasons why they were in politics
must be explained and in this way it will be possible to
show what politics meant to them and to foresee how they
would use their power.

At least a third of all the M.P.s of the reign were born
into politics, and their parents had occupied positions
equivalent or superior to their own ; but the attitudes of
these men, the amount of support they would give the
government, and what they expected to get out of politics
differed greatly.   The heirs of the great names of the first
empire sat in parliament as though by hereditary right.
Sometimes they were the junior members of a family, and
had to be content with a seat in the legislature while their
seniors sat in the senate ; others were there simply because
they could not be accommodated in the senate.   They
were the ornaments of the house and not the pillars of the
régime, for few of them were powerful in their constituencies, and though they would support the empire with
their votes, they brought it little independent strength.
Their presence, however, was not an isolated concession
to the memory of the past, for nepotism still flourished as a
vigorous institution.   The Murat family, for example, held
royal sway over the department of Lot.   First, therefore,
the M.P. for Lot was Lafon de Cayx, a retired prefect,
nephew of King Murat ; and on his death Joachim Murat,

[1] Taillefer, ACL 1861, 1. 313-14.

51

a member of the younger branch, succeeded him to hold the seat for thirty-five years (1854–89). The department was represented by two M.P.s, and when the second one died, he was replaced by Denat, the son-in-law of Lafon de Cayx, who was a retired judge. The ministers and the great men of the régime likewise had their relations in the lower house : Baroche put in his brother-in-law to preserve his influence in Versailles, the ministers Vuitry, Billault, Magne, Delangle, Magnan and Haussmann all had their sons-in-law in it. The sons of Fould and of La Valette and the nephew of Schneider (president of the legislature), also had seats found for them.[1] Half of these, however, were men of real personal worth.

The tendency to make politics the preserve of a few families was even more noticeable in the seventeen instances of M.P.s being succeeded by their sons, nephews, sons-in-law or brothers.[2] This system had its merits as well as its dangers. It enabled families to found Bonapartist dynasties with great influence in various parts of the country ; and it was one way of opening the doors of parliament to young men. But, of course, it also limited the range of support to which the régime could appeal and it drove otherwise loyal men into the ranks of the opposition when they saw no hope of getting a seat under such conditions. Nepotism was, however, in no way confined to the second empire : it flourished as is well known in the preceding régimes, and even the republicans were as guilty of it as anybody else. The opposition candidates of the period contain many obscure names whose main importance was that they were nephews or sons-in-law of this or that leader.

Some dynasties of parliamentarians were so firmly established before 1852 that their representatives came to

---

[1] Delapalme, Welles, Quesné, Busson, Desseiligny, Germain, Gaudin, Haentjens, Dollfus.

[2] Vast-Vimeux, Villedieu, Rolle, Reille, Gorsse, Kersaint, Guistière, Corneille, André, Simon, Cambacérès, Gellibert, Daguilhon-Pujol, Bois, Rotours, Mouchy, Lefebure.

sit in the house as though politics was always the same for
them. They were M.P.s though kings might come and go.
These dynasties varied greatly in character. A few were
of imperial origin, and though they sat happily enough
under other governments, the re-establishment of the
empire revived their loyalty and their children would stand
in the third republic as Bonapartists. A few had no connection with Bonapartism, but were converted to it. A
good example of this type is Taillefer, son of an M.P. of the
revolution and M.P. himself (with a two years' break)
from 1846 to 1868. To begin with, he said after the liberal
changes of 1860, 'I supported the empire because I was
convinced that it alone could save France. Now I will
support it from taste and with affection, because I like it.
I like it because it has restored to me my dignity as a
citizen by making me participate in the conduct of the
affairs of my country.'[1] His son was in due course Bonapartist member for the same constituency after the fall of
the empire.

Though some ancient families were converted to Bonapartism, it was more frequent for men to set greater store
on preserving their own dynasty in their department than
another's in Paris. They preferred to change their politics
and to move with the times. Boissy d'Anglas' father, a
lawyer of Ardèche, had entered parliament in 1789 and
had become senator of the empire and peer of the restoration. He himself became M.P. in 1828; he started by
opposing Polignac and then sat loyally in the Orleanist
majority. In 1852 he returned for twelve more years,
again a supporter of the *de facto* government. His son
succeeded him in 1877 as a republican and opportunist.
Another example is the son of a bodyguard of Charles X,
M.P. and peer under Louis Philippe; the nephew of a
bishop and related to a M.P. of 1789, to a gentleman-in-
ordinary to the king, to a baron of the empire, and to a

[1] ACL 1861, 1. 313-14.

peer. He had the tastes of a wealthy young man accustomed to luxury and ease. 'For him politics are a matter of personal interest and of fashion, and not a question of developing methodically and solidly the enlightenment or the liberty of a people.'[1] Such types moved with the times and they, moreover, would not be henchmen of absolutism.

These men, who were given seats by famous relations or who inherited them from their fathers, were what may be called politicians of the second generation, who merely kept up an inherited status. Now, how did men get up to this rank in the first generation ? A few made great names for themselves and won their seats the direct way ; but the more common method of advancement was through long service to the state, which frequently extended several generations back. Little jobs led to bigger jobs, and big jobs brought good marriages which doubled a man's influence and frequently opened the way into parliament for him or his children. Mège, who was minister in 1870, is a good example. His father was a solicitor who rose to be a judge of the peace and who married the daughter of a judge. He himself started as barrister and married the daughter of the local principal controller of direct taxation. It was probably as much through their influence as through his own remarkable ability that he became a deputy judge, then mayor of Clermont-Ferrand and so its M.P.[2] Dugué de La Fauconnerie was the grandson of a 'general administrator' of the revolution, the grand-nephew of a member of the convention and sub-prefect of the Hundred Days ; and his family had held many offices in the administration and the magistracy. Now he became engaged to the daughter of the prefect of his department, was given a job in his office, then made a prefectoral counsellor and got married on the strength of it. He thus became a cousin of

---

[1] F(1b) I 167 (26), Le Sergeant de Monnecove's file, prefects' reports, 2.4.1852 and 5.11.1853.   [2] BB(6) II 291, his file.

Baron Jerome David, and, with this strong support, was appointed a sub-prefect. He made his mark by organising the defeat of a clerical M.P. whom the government threw out in 1863, and was decorated for it with the Legion of Honour. In 1869 he entered parliament and remained there for many years.[1] Boucaumont was the son of a director of the domains, the nephew of a general who was a M.P., and the cousin of a magistrate who was also a M.P. He was educated at the Polytechnic, and served for almost forty years in the department of Public Works (*Ponts et Chaussées*), nearly all of them in one department. He rose to be chief engineer and acquired great influence and respect for his ability. In 1863 he entered parliament.[2]

Now if jobs in the service of the state frequently gave an entry into politics, how did completely new men, who had no influence to back them, get into these jobs? The main path was through the professions and especially through the law. It is a great mistake to label a parliament as 'bourgeois' because it is full of barristers. The law was by long tradition the method by which the bourgeoisie rose to nobility. Barristers had become judges and had founded dynasties of judges in the provincial courts of the *ancien régime*. Any young man of wealth with no particular vocation would study law, for a degree in it was essential for entry into a great many state jobs. Thus a M.P. wrote: 'My position and my territorial wealth have constantly obliged me to cultivate the study of law',[3] showing how law in nineteenth-century France still held much the same place as it had in seventeenth-century England, when the country gentlemen crowded the Inns of Court. There were many lawyers in parliament but few plain barristers with no family backing. The barristers who were elected were normally men who had risen to the front rank at their

[1] F(1b) I 158(33), his file.
[2] F(14) 2177(1), his file and also his brother's.
[3] F(1c) II 98, Ardennes file, Piette to minister of the Interior, 23.1.1852.

provincial bars, who had been elected presidents of their local corporations of barristers (*bâtonnier de l'ordre*) ; who had served their towns as mayors and who, having given proof of their ability in politics and administration, were sent to represent them in Paris. The opposition had a large proportion of barristers amongst them, simply because they were excluded from offices by their opposition. They got their jobs in due course after the fall of the empire.

There was another method of entering politics without influence, and that was through the army. Here again the army was a fashionable career, and many young men went into it for a few years before retiring to their country estates. But no less numerous were the men who, having worked their way up to the rank of colonel or general, were not illustrious enough on the national scale to be appointed to the senate, but who were nevertheless the glory of their departments. A retired general thus frequently went into parliament to end his days : to rise occasionally to praise the valour of the forces in war, perhaps to urge some reform in military equipment, but generally to represent in silence the conservatism of merit rewarded.

The characteristic which distinguishes the parliamentarians of the second empire is the relatively large number of them engaged in trade, industry and finance. These occupations were, on the whole, the preserves of new men of humble or middle class origin who had taken no part in politics, and who were therefore free to join these parliaments. Such men were the brothers Isaac and Jacob-Émile Pereire, sons of a teacher, who had become magnates in the great new forces of credit banks and railways. Merchants making fortunes in the main ports of France, pioneers of great factories of iron and textile, bankers, leading printers and speculative newspaper owners rising on the tide of popular reading, owners too of old but large distilleries and factories of porcelain or textile : there were many of these.

They were seldom very absorbed by politics. One, a banker, M.P. for thirty-six years until he became senator, was proud to say that he had hardly spoken except on finance, and had avoided 'political preoccupations'.[1] Their hearts were in their businesses. They came to parliament to put their experience at the service of the state and to defend their interests, which were very much dependent on government policy. Some, it is true, were conscious of their origins, proud of the new forces they stood for, and, like the printer Laroche-Joubert, became staunch Bonapartists. Some were not even new men at all. There were old aristocrats who owned mines; many a politician of a former government expelled by revolution had gone into industry; not a few were men who had reached parliament by other means and had then begun to dabble in finance and railway concessions — among whom Morny was perhaps the classic example and the peer.

Schneider shows the sort of men these industrialists were, though he is outstanding rather than typical. The son of a notary, he served his apprenticeship in a bank and as manager of a local iron factory. Then with his brother as the financier and negotiator, and himself as the engineer (taught by practice and not by theory), he laid the foundations of the great organisation of Le Creusot, which became the leading producer of locomotives, steel rails, machinery and arms in France. His brother Adolphe had married the daughter of an iron master and M.P., and himself went to represent in parliament the constituency in which Le Creusot stood. When Adolphe died, Eugène succeeded him in his seat and held it from 1845 to 1848 and from 1852 to 1870. He became minister of Agriculture and Commerce during the presidency of Louis Napoleon, and then president of the legislature in 1867. He was a man of business and not a politician: his great achievement in his eyes was not his high offices, but the immense industrial organisation

[1] CRCL 1855, 585-6, Gouin.

he had established. One day, as he was presiding over the house, a telegram was brought to him and on reading it his face lit up with uncontrollable pleasure. Trembling with joy, he announced that never before had he had such a happy moment; he had just won a contract to sell locomotives to England, 'to England', he repeated to the applause of the house. Such were the real sources of satisfaction and the real goals of ambition for these pioneers.[1]

Finally, there was a large group of members who were landowners. Sometimes they devoted themselves actively to pioneering new methods, to draining marshes and establishing model farms, and they could thus be regarded as the ablest representatives of the agricultural interest, even though this type seldom owned very wide acres. Others, however, were mere gentlemen of leisure, with no real occupation, who were glad to have the use of a desirable club in Paris when they came up for the season. Probably every single M.P. was a landowner of sorts. There is no French word for 'gentleman'. The French equivalent to it, which a man would use after his name when he wished to show he had no occupation, is *propriétaire*. No great wealth is necessary to become a *propriétaire*, and it is, of course, every Frenchman's ambition to be one. There must have been few M.P.s who did not inherit some land. Their political status gave them strong motives for buying some in the constituencies they represented, as men from the provinces who had settled in Paris very frequently did. But there must have been few, too, who had no property except in land; for, quite apart from the normal attractions of stocks and shares, M.P.s frequently took a financial interest in local railways and similar enterprises in their constituencies to increase their political influence. Marriage with money was not uncommon either: indeed, the careers of some M.P.s suggest that this was a golden age

[1] M. Eugène Boyer's manuscript life of Schneider, Schneider papers.

of rich heiresses. Suchet, duc d'Albufera, son of the marshal, married the daughter of the Prussian banker Schickler. Calvet-Rogniat, nephew of the minister Capelle, adopted by the sister of General Rogniat, married the daughter of Jaoul, one of the richest manufacturers of Normandy. Conversely, St-Paul, M.P., banker, director of many railways and mines, married off his two daughters, one to General Fleury, senator and aide-de-camp to H.M., and the other to Bugeaud, duc d'Isly. The comte de Chambrun married the daughter of Godard-Desmarets, a fellow M.P., and owner of the glass factory of Baccarat.[1]

The only men who were politicians first and foremost were perhaps the journalists. The greatest of these was Granier de Cassagnac, a man of great vigour of speech and conviction, with a career full of polemic, duels and invective, the picador of the liberal bulls, the staunchest of Bonapartists. Entering journalism on leaving school, he went to Paris after the revolution of 1830 with a letter of introduction to his local M.P., Remusat. By him he was brought to the notice of Guizot, under whose patronage he established his reputation as a lively and vigorous writer in the conservative cause. In 1848 he supported Louis Napoleon and from then, founding or buying various papers to be his instruments, he became the leading journalist in the defence of the empire. Elected to parliament in 1852, he built up a tremendous influence in his constituency and held his seat (with a break between 1870 and 1876) till his death in 1880, to be succeeded by his son, a journalist of no less energy and talent.[2]

It can now be seen that the M.P.s of the second empire

---

[1] Robert et Cougny, *Dictionnaire des parlementaires français*. G. Vapereau, *Dictionnaire des contemporains* (1880 edition). A. Poulet-Malassis, *Papiers secrets et correspondance du second empire*, 65. F(1c) II 98, Aveyron, prefect, 29.1.1852. É. Ollivier, *L'Empire libéral*, 4. 72.

[2] Robert et Cougny, *op. cit.* ; Taschereau, *Revue rétrospective*, 271-2 ; Granier de Cassagnac, *Souvenirs* ; J. Dagnan, *Le Gers sous la seconde république*, 154-5, 364 ff. A. Poulet-Malassis, *Papiers secrets et correspondance du second empire* (1880), 48. Information from M. Paul de Cassagnac.

were no puppets of the government, but men with a standing of their own, with individual careers, ambitions and aims, for whom the dynasty was not everything and from whom permanent and unswerving support could not be expected. Indeed it was not in the government's interest to pack parliaments with nonentities. Dr. Conneau, Napoleon's physician from the days of Ham, was made member for the constituency in which that prison lay, for it was the only place with which he could be said to have any association ; but this was a unique case and a sort of joke. He was an unsatisfactory M.P., who hardly ever visited his constituency, never answered letters and built up no influence in the government's favour.[1] Moreover, a M.P. who was too Bonapartist was inconvenient ; for service demands reward and Napoleon was lucky that he did not come into power with more sheep than he had pasture on which to feed them. This is illustrated in the career of Belmontet, a Bonapartist since the restoration, a companion of exile of Queen Hortense and of Louis Napoleon, author of much propaganda and poetry on their behalf, the man who introduced Persigny to them. He was M.P. for his native department throughout the empire. Now he was perpetually making demands for jobs for his friends, and for decorations for himself, as acknowledgements of his great services to the cause. In parliament he was one of the most uncontrollable of members. He got up, for example, to oppose the government's proposal to prosecute Montalembert, saying that he had no fear of being accused of opposing the government : 'Thirty-five years of struggle for the Napoleonic idea makes any justification unnecessary for him'. There is a letter from Napoleon to him which shows Napoleon's attitude to this. 'My dear M. Belmontet,' it reads, 'I have received your request for an audience and I write to tell you why I am not granting it to you. Ever since I have been at the head of the govern-

---

[1] BB(30) 427, *procureur général*, Amiens, 19.5.1863.

ment, your language both in Paris and in the provinces has been so inconsistent with the truth that I cannot countenance the opinions you have expressed by receiving you. I am very grateful for the devotion you have always shown me, but I cannot allow you to pass yourself off as my intimate confidant and as the secret agent of my wishes. . . . I very much regret that your thoughtless conduct has prevented me for many years from giving you proofs of my old friendship. . . .'[1]

These men, moreover, were not in parliament to make money. There is an old belief that the empire was a 'racket' with political power exploited by adventurers for financial gain. Napoleon himself, however, died leaving little more than he had inherited. Persigny married Ney's granddaughter and was given a dowry of half a million francs (£20,000) by Napoleon; and that was about the amount he left his son on his death. Billault built his château with the proceeds of his wife's dowry and his own provincial practice, before he entered politics. When he was appointed president of the legislature in 1852, accepting was a financial sacrifice for him, for he had been earning 80,000 francs a year as one of Paris's leading barristers. In 1861 Napoleon bought him a fully furnished house in Paris for 600,000 francs on his appointment as minister without portfolio: when Billault died he left this, his own château, and very little else. Morny no doubt speculated actively, but he probably spent more than he earned. Forcade la Roquette once said: 'The enemies of the empire claim that we fatten ourselves at the expense of the people. Well, I had an income of 300,000 francs and after having been minister five times, I have got only 25,000.' It is certain that his widow left only 380,588 francs capital.

[1] Napoleon to Belmontet, copy, Billault papers. A. Poulet-Malassis, *Papiers secrets et correspondance du second empire* (1880), 306-8, 335 ; CRCL 1854, 57-8 and 337-40 ; ACL 1861, 2. 9-11 ; ACL 1862, 4. 19 ; ACL 1868, 4. 157-63 ; F(1c) II 102, Tarn-et-Garonne file ; Belmontet to Napoleon, 20.3.1852, Billault papers.

Émile Ollivier and Chasseloup-Laubat, both men of perfect integrity and of the highest principles, certainly did not use politics to enrich themselves. The latter, for example, sold his shares on becoming minister in 1859; and in 1869, as president of the council of state, refused to draw his salary of 30,000 francs. These instances, which research has unearthed, seem to prove that in this period one did not make money by becoming minister. Other cases, relating to plain M.P.s, show how even a provincial barrister lost financially by giving up his practice for politics.[1] It is true that M.P.s were frequently offered free shares by companies anxious to have their support in parliament; but on the other hand, they had the expense of living in Paris for part of the year; they were expected to be generous to charity; and as politics became more controversial, they often had to subsidise newspapers and other forms of electoral propaganda.

The M.P.s can be divided roughly according to their occupations in this way:

109 are known to have been landowners [2]		about 19%
98 former civil servants		
14 officers of the royal household		
39 former members of the legal civil service		about 26%
5 former members of the *Ponts et Chaussées*		
2 former members of the department of mines		
75 industrialists		
4 engineers		
2 printers		
22 financiers		about 24%
33 merchants		
1 worker		

[1] B.N., Δ 30894, p.72. H. de Laire to his father about Persigny, 9.5. and 30.7.1872, Persigny papers. Notes in Billault papers and letter of Billault to Mocquard, 20.9.1859 in Billault papers. Meynis de Paulin papers. J. Delarbre, *Chasseloup-Laubat* (1873), 15; notes in Chasseloup papers. Segris papers. F(1c) II 98, prefect of Côte-d'Or on Vernier, 27.1.1852.

[2] Landowners without any other profession.

67 barristers	
12 notaries	} about 13%
2 solicitors	
14 doctors	
17 writers	
8 teachers	} about 7%
3 artists	
51 soldiers	about 8%
7 mayors otherwise unclassifiable	—

Now there are two great differences between these figures and those for the monarchy of July. First, civil servants were now excluded from parliament whereas they had formerly comprised from 32 to 45 per cent of the M.P.s.[1] This certainly widened the basis of Napoleon's recruitment. The large number of former civil servants, by the way, shows how parliament and the civil service continued to be closely linked and how both were very similar channels for political ambition. Secondly, the number of industrialists, merchants and financiers under the second empire was far larger than, for example, in 1836 (10 per cent) or in 1848 (14 per cent).[2] There were also far fewer writers, professors, teachers and intellectuals and fewer barristers than in 1848. The parliaments of Napoleon contained almost as many new men as that of 1848, but more of them had already made their mark in practical affairs.

It is now clear what the occupations of the M.P.s were, but there is a great deal of difference within these occupations, and a 'merchant' may well be either the owner of a few shops or the head of a vast commercial organisation. What rank therefore did these men have in society ? Were they the leading and richest men of their respective classes,

[1] S. Charlety, *La Monarchie de juillet* 347 ; cf. Gaugier in M.U. 1841, 900.

[2] *Ibid.* and A. Chaboseau in *La Révolution de 1848*, vol. 7, 295-305, 413-25.

or were the leaders already pledged to legitimism or Orleanism? The answer is that they included men of all rank and wealth. It has been possible to discover the private incomes of sixty-five members: their accuracy cannot be checked nor are they a representative sample in any way. However, they show that

```
18 or about 28% had 10,000 francs or less (about £400)
24 or about 37% had 11-20,000 francs (£440-800)
 8 or about 12% had 21-30,000 francs (£840-1200)
 4 or about  6% had 31-40,000 francs (£1240-1600)
 3 or about  5% had 41-50,000 francs (£1640-2000)
 6 or about  9% had 51-100,000 francs (£2040-4000)
 2 or about  3% had over 100,000 francs (£4040)
```

Here are some more detailed specimens of incomes. Baroche's brother-in-law, the notary Delapalme, owned about a thousand acres. An industrialist had a capital of six to seven millions which yielded an income of 30,000 francs. One of the members for Tarn was the richest landowner of that department. His father had made a great fortune during the empire and then obtained the lucrative post of receiver-general at Bordeaux. He married the daughter of the Marshal de Pérignon, and bequeathed 200,000 francs a year to his son, the M.P., who was thus able to spend a great deal of money on local good works.[1] An obscure M.P. of Ain owned about two thousand acres, from which he derived an income of 25,000-30,000 francs.[2] Dowries were very considerable: two former civil servants doubled their incomes by marriage, and another two quadrupled theirs.[3] A lawyer of Aix earned 15,000 francs a year from his practice; he had 20,000 a year from investments and the mine-owner's daughter whom he had married would inherit an equal income. He had his

---

[1] F(1c) II 102, prefect, 6.2.1852 on Carayon-Latour; his speeches, M.U. 1847, 3010, 1598 and 2990; M.U. 1848, 226; M.U. 1849, 419.
[2] F(1c) II 98, prefect, 6.2.1852. Bodin.
[3] Fremy and Houdetot; Lequien and Chambrun.

parliamentary salary of 7500 francs and an expense allowance from his town of 3000.[1]

The equal division of inherited property among children and the great preponderance of small peasant ownership of the land made the accumulation of large estates difficult. The practice was for a property to be divided among children but then recombined by marriage and so to be perpetually reconstituted in different hands. Nevertheless, it is clear that the M.P.s were not the richest men of France, though they included quite a few who were. They were especially not the greatest landowners, who were generally legitimists. There were many leading industrialists among them, but no doubt as many who had made their money too late were excluded. The new men of the second empire grew old in their turn and the republic recruited the very new men of the 1860s.

[1] BB(6) II 366, Rigaud's file, note in his handwriting, *c.* 1855. The original constitution of 14 January 1852 gave no salary to the members of the legislature. The sénatus-consulte of 25 December 1852, however, gave them a salary of 2500 francs for each month during which parliament was in session.

CHAPTER V

How the election of 1857 encouraged a conservative reaction

ANOTHER general election was held in 1857. It was a quiet affair, the government and the opposition got almost exactly the same number of votes as in 1852, and it is usual therefore to dismiss it all as an event of little interest and of less consequence. In fact the identical figures conceal a great change. In 1852 the opposition was, above all, legitimist, but in 1857 it was nearly all republican. Its quietness was the most important thing about it, because these republican votes were obtained with very little electioneering, rather like subscriptions being collected from old members of a club. The election, furthermore, shows the government already faced with many of the problems which were to burden it in its later struggles. In many ways therefore the year 1857 ought to be regarded as a prominent landmark in the development of the second empire.

The position of the government was like that of an old pugilist who had many years before risen conclusively above all rivals, and whose prowess had for long been unquestioned. He must, now and again, confirm his supremacy. Every little success against him will seem immense ; his achievements have become a legend and he alone remembers the narrow margins of his victories. He knows that if he is compelled to perform, he will not show himself as prodigious as he is made out to be, and his real hope is that no one will dare to challenge him. It was in such a spirit that the government prepared for the fight.

The control of the campaign was in the hands of

Billault, who had been minister of the Interior since 1854. He is an interesting man and all the more so because he is one of the stock types of Napoleon III's servants. Morny used to say that the reactionaries and the conservatives of the second empire were the men who were liberal under Louis Philippe, and that the true liberals of the empire were those who had, like himself, been conservatives under Louis Philippe.[1] There is much truth in this view, for ardent reformers frequently have the reputation of being liberal until they begin to put their theories into practice. Billault illustrates the problem well. He was of middle class stock; his grandfathers were both lawyers; his father was a senior customs official, disgraced by the restoration for his co-operation with Napoleon I. He himself, more endowed with intelligence and energy than with wealth, became a barrister at Nantes at 20, a member of its municipal council and the son-in-law of one of its richest ship-owners at 25. With the backing of this influence behind him, he was a member of parliament as soon as his age allowed it; and such was his success that he was an under-secretary within a few years. He rose to be one of the leading barristers of Paris, and built himself a château outside Nantes. In politics he sat first near Barrot, then near Thiers, and finally formed a group of independents of the left which included Tocqueville, Bineau, Lanjuinais, Abbatucci, Drouyn, all of whom became ministers of Napoleon. Unlike Barrot and Thiers, his main interest was in social affairs. This theme, which runs through his life, helps to explain his apparent tergiversations and his conversion from an Orleanist liberal into a conservative Bonapartist.

In 1834 he wrote, 'The sole aim worthy of effort in politics is the moral and material amelioration of the country, and really the two parties seem to have entirely forgotten it'.[2] The state, he said in 1848, cannot abstain

---

[1] Montalembert's diary, 4. and 14.4.1856.
[2] Billault's works, 1. 169.

from the social life of the people. He opposed the *laisser-faire* policy of Louis Philippe and insisted on the necessity of state intervention in economic questions.[1] The thread of his development is clear when, well seated in power, he wrote, 'There was need to know how to be at once very liberal in foreign policy, and at home very preoccupied with popular improvements, but not submissive before the pretensions of the little oligarchy of writers and self-styled statesmen who take the soap bubbles of their own speeches to be free government. To speak little, to do much, ought to be the motto of the Napoleons, just as to speak much and to do nothing was, if not the motto, at least the practice of the government of 1830.'[2] After 1848 he enjoyed considerable popularity with the left for his reforming ideas; and the red terror which followed did not turn him into a blind reactionary. 'What I ask for our country', he wrote in December 1849, 'is a strong and resolute government, respected at home and also abroad, which, while guaranteeing us peace in the street, knows how to make the best of all wars against subversive ideas, that is to effect without hesitations, for the benefit of the people, all really practicable improvements.'[3] Few men, however, became Bonapartists for purely theoretical reasons; what converted Billault finally was the attraction of Napoleon's personality, the kindness he received at his hands and the high opinion he formed of his ability.[4] Napoleon may have won the masses by his name and his principles, but he frequently won their political leaders by his own personal qualities.

In such hands the election could be expected to follow much the same lines as that of 1852. Billault was well aware of the difficulties. The election, he wrote to the emperor, could not be as easy as that of 1852. Then all

[1] M.U. 1848, 2450-1.
[2] Billault to Princess Roccagiovine, *c.* 1862, Billault papers.
[3] Profession of faith, Billault papers.
[4] Billault to Tharréou, *conseiller de préfecture*, Loire-Inf., 10.1 1851, 5.2.1851, 18.12.1851, Billault papers.

had been dominated by the great success of a plebiscite: now they must expect some demagogues to be elected by the workers in the large towns; and the legitimists and Orleanists to wage a silent war, not openly putting up their own candidates, but hiding behind apparently harmless candidates. The attitude of the clergy was uncertain. The government must accordingly make sure of all 'legitimate means of influence. It is necessary at all costs that the people should not be able to say either in France or in Europe, that the imperial government has lost ground with the masses.'[1]

As before, he declared, all could stand for parliament, but the official candidates would be supported with all the means in the government's power. 'The government cannot alone remain dumb and indifferent. It will tell the country which men have its confidence. . . .' To the prefects he wrote, 'You will give them your patronage openly and you will fight without hesitation all candidatures, not only those which announce themselves as being hostile, but even those which claim they are devoted. . . . You will give the candidates of the administration all possible facilities, official and semi-official.'[2] Whom was the government to choose as official candidates? If it chose the sitting M.P.s, it would close its ranks to the many men willing to rally if given a chance, and drive youthful talent into opposition. It decided, none the less, that it could not throw these old M.P.s away, who had, after all, supported it faithfully. But what of those who had shown independence and had voted against the government? Here Billault acted without any systematic principles. The men of substance who could lead and sustain, who had taken a foremost part in opposition in the last session, and who were to direct it in later ones — these were for the most part left

[1] Billault to Napoleon, draft, 9.11.1856, Billault papers.
[2] Billault to Napoleon, draft, 9.11.1856, Billault papers; Heeckeren to Persigny, 6.12.1856, Persigny papers; circular in A.D. Côte-d'Or, 3 M 72, 30.5.1857; very confidential circular, 1.6.1857, *ibid*.

alone. The local position of some was too strong; they were there indeed very often because the government had thought them inevitable in 1852; or else they had ties of influence which made their positions in Paris strong.

In any case, Montalembert alone of the leaders was abandoned. His opposition had made his situation impossible. On a visit to his constituency in 1856, he had found everybody personally kind, but 'icily cold on politics. No-one says anything to encourage me to hope for a re-election and even Nicod does not hide from me the difficulty which the clergy will have to fight for me against the government.' Montalembert had an old alliance with a local newspaper, which continued to support him. The clergy, however, would not help him because he was opposed by the government. All the same, the government, underestimating its own strength, established a newspaper of its own to fight him, with a salaried editor sent from Paris. Yet even though its candidate was an obscure chamberlain with none of Montalembert's brilliant qualities, it defeated him by 17,000 to 4000.[1] Some eight obscure M.P.s[2] whose opposition had been confined to occasional votes, were likewise deprived of official patronage, but the fact of their opposition played only a limited part in the decision. For the prefects often claimed that the position of certain M.P.s was unsatisfactory, and that their re-election would be very difficult.[3] Several of these men put up inefficacious resistance and were easily defeated: by dint of extraordinary energy only a couple managed to survive.

Then the government was faced with the problem of Durfort de Civrac, who, after allowing it to distribute his ballot papers for a month, suddenly disclaimed his status

[1] Montalembert's diary, 24.8.1856; Montalembert to Flavigny (copies), 1.1.1857 and 29.6.1857, Montalembert papers.

[2] Montreuil, Leroy-Beaulieu, David, Desmolles, Charlier, Levavasseur, Migeon, Rambourgt.

[3] *E.g.* F(90) 347, Eure, telegrams of 22-25.5.1857; F(90) 588, telegrams of 20 and 25.5.1857.

of official candidate and announced himself independent. He was opposed, and, after an agitated struggle, defeated. It was an important victory, for Durfort de Civrac was a legitimist, and the success of a Bonapartist in this old *chouan* stronghold was significant, even though the legitimists were responsible for it themselves. The government celebrated by promoting the local sub-prefect.[1]

It was, however, defeated more often than is realised. Several independents were elected who have been forgotten because their opposition was not very marked. Curé, an independent liberal, elected in Bordeaux, was later won over by free trade. Javal, a Jewish industrialist and financier, became a conservative republican after 1870. Jules Brame, an agriculturalist of Lille, more conservative than the preceding two, was minister in 1870, when he formed a friendship with the empress which turned him into a Bonapartist. Two others (Morgan and Halligon), rich men with sufficient Orleanist antecedents to make them oppose the official candidates, were also elected, though they generally supported the government in parliament. Other independents might also have got in, had they not, like the duc d'Uzès, voluntarily withdrawn.

Finally there was the case of Plichon, an able speaker of liberal views, whose influential friends had secured him the support of the government. But he refused to promise support to the government in return. The campaign in his favour had gone so far that the prefect thought that his election was inevitable; no-one would stand against him. The government was therefore forced to accept him without any written assurances.[2]

Eight independents were thus elected to parliament in 1857, in addition to the famous five republicans. It was, however, from the republicans that the really important

---

[1] A.D. M.-&-L. 8M50; F(1c) III, M.-&-L. 8, sub-prefect, Beaupreau, 1.7.1857; BB(18)1567, *procureur général*, Angers, 6.6.1857–11.7.1857; note in Billault papers.
[2] F(90) 347, 12 and 15.6.1857.

opposition came. Since 1852 they had remained stunned in silence and inactivity. How ought they to act now? Ought they to vote or abstain? Ought the men who succeeded in getting elected take the oath and sit in parliament? Ought they to ally with the Orleanists and legitimists? The delegations of workers who spoke to the leaders were generally in favour of abstention, for they felt certain that they would be defeated. Those in favour of action did not contradict this belief but claimed simply that it was a matter of duty to vote: had not the empire been founded the day Louis Napoleon had landed at Boulogne with his eagle, even though his adventure had miscarried? But, cried the opponents, our small vote will merely strengthen the empire. No, replied the others, for our aim is to do as the sailor, who drops his sounding lead to discover how much water he has beneath him. In the end, the republicans decided to vote, though they did not determine their action on other problems.[1]

There followed a campaign with two important characteristics, only the first of which has been appreciated. The division of the republicans between the old and the new men and their putting up two different lists is well known. It was all really due to Havin, the political director of the *Siècle*, a paper with immense power. The old gang refused him the constituency he wanted. In anger he seceded and published in his paper a list of candidates of his own choosing. The old republicans were thus superseded not by the strength of the young, but by their own lack of tact; and it was the arrival of this youthful group which produced the rejuvenation of the republican party. But equally important was the second outstanding characteristic of the election. The policy of not abstaining was carried into the provinces. From Paris a circular was distributed urging the republicans to put up as many candidates as possible. If there are any

[1] Ollivier's diary, 25.11.1856 and 25.5.1857.

local democratic candidates in your department, it read, whose past services distinguish them and whose success is likely, support them ; if not, choose from among the M.P.s of 1848 those you consider most popular. Do not fear to compromise these names by failure or by their getting only a small number of votes. The ambitious may fear defeat, but those devoted to the cause can sustain it with honour. Ledru-Rollin from London sent a flaming circular headed, 'No abstention ; you must vote'. The forgotten shades of the reds of 1848 sprang to life. The local organisers chose their prefects or M.P.s of 1848, while some preferred to choose a great name, which enabled them to proclaim the nuance of republicanism that pleased them most. A dozen chose Cavaignac, five Carnot, a few Garnier-Pagès, Lamartine or Raspail. Ledru-Rollin's old secretary stood in Corrèze, Felix Pyat's nephew in Cher.[1]

Apart from the encouragement to fight the election, no practical help came from Paris ; and there was very little organisation in the constituencies themselves. It was all the work of a few enthusiasts, working without resources. In Dordogne 40,000 ballot papers were written out by hand. The invitation to vote was passed around discreetly by a few scattered conspirators. This is what makes the result important, that so little effort should have got such a large vote of about half a million. Furthermore, these half million votes did not represent the full republican strength. In many departments they were left without candidates of their own and were therefore forced to abstain. In the undoubtedly republican manufacturing town of Decazeville, for example, only 640 out of 3009 electors voted.[2]

---

[1] BB(18) 1567, sent by *procureur général*, Rouen, 1.5.1857 ; *ibid.*, *procureur général*, Limoges, 12.6.1857 ; *ibid.*, *procureur général*, Bourges, 17.6.1857.

[2] *Ibid.*, *procureur général*, Bordeaux, 20.6.1857 ; *ibid.*, *procureur impérial*, Domfront, 23.6.1857 ; A.D. Aveyron, 1857 election file, prefect, 2.7.1857.

There were republican candidates in about a hundred constituencies, but only a bare handful of legitimists stood, and a mere dozen men of Orleanist antecedents, in addition to the usual sprinkling of dissident Bonapartists, candidates representing local rivalries and about thirty whose politics are uncertain. All these were small men. None of the leaders of the legitimists or Orleanists stood. It is clear that they believed that they stood no chance. It was not that they thought that it was not worth joining a parliament with such limited powers. Montalembert wrote to Flavigny that he believed that the legislature could, if it wanted to, play a very important part in politics. Buffet justified his candidature thus : the legislature, he said, had less power than its predecessors, but 'its rights can be widened and it is assuredly permissible to suppose that the state of public opinion, the new glory our arms have acquired, the honourable peace which has ended a national war, bring near the moment when the constitutional framework will be crowned with the liberty which its author has promised'.[1] These men, however, were the exceptions. The old leaders did nothing.

The figures of the election results were almost identical with those of 1852. 65 per cent of the electorate voted, as against 63 per cent in 1852. The government got 84·6 per cent of these votes as compared with 83 per cent, and the opposition 13·6 per cent as compared with 13 per cent. But though the totals are the same, the distribution is very different. In 1852 the opposition had been strongest in the west. Now in Loire-Inférieure, in Finistère and in Ille-et-Vilaine, the government's vote doubled, and in other western departments and in Pas-de-Calais there were also extraordinarily large increases (Côtes-du-Nord, Vendée, Sèvres, Morbihan). On the other hand, its vote fell in many departments in the eastern half of France, as

---

[1] Montalembert to Flavigny, 27.11.1857, Montalembert papers, copy ; BB(18) 1567, *procureur général*, Nancy, on Vosges.

well as in the departments which were later to become Bonapartist, viz., Gironde, the Charentes and Dordogne. These changes are of the greatest importance. A mere comparison of the results of 1852 and 1869 would show the same gains in the west, but they would be attributed to the legitimists joining forces with the government for the sake of 'order' against the menace of the red revolution. In 1857 there was no such menace. The legitimists openly declared themselves hostile to the empire and counselled abstention. These increases therefore represent, not a union with foreign allies, but the Bonapartists' own proper gains.

The reaction of the government to the elections was more varied than is realised. Napoleon was, on the whole, not dissatisfied. 'I was very surprised', he telegraphed to the minister of State, 'to see the summary of the general elections inserted in a corner of the *Moniteur*, like some statistic, instead of being put in large letters on the first page.' 'The difference between 1852 and 1857', he wrote to Billault, 'is very good and ought to be pointed out. I am pleased to recognise that your zeal and your enlightened direction were not stranger to the success obtained. I am very much of your opinion. Far from falling asleep, we must on the contrary seek to discover how we could fight the evil disposition of the great towns. Be very severe towards the press and point out to me as well as to your colleagues the officials who did not do their duty.'[1]

The ministers were less impressed by the huge total majority than by the strength of the republicans in the towns and the danger it boded for the future.[2] Billault's report to the emperor particularly stressed this point. The election had shown, he said, that despite all that the emperor had done in these last five years to improve the

---

[1] F(90) 499, 6.7.1857 ; Napoleon to Billault, copy, 29.6.1857, Billault papers.   [2] Cf. Fould to Baroche, 16.7.1857, Bibl. Thiers, 989 f. 35.

lot of the workers, they had not changed but had merely kept quiet from fear of superior force. The government must therefore continue to keep them down. The most urgent problem was that of Paris, whose population could not be cured, and which must therefore be reduced in size and deprived of its character of an industrial town.[1]

Haussmann sent Napoleon a long report supporting Billault. 'No good can be hoped for from this population without religious or moral principles, half educated, greedy of pleasure. . . . Many people who believe they are exorcising the danger by refusing to see it, will try to explain our electoral defeat [in Paris] by petty causes. They will say that, to calm the evil passions which still exist, we must make some concession, grant more liberty, administer with increasing gentleness. They will counsel above all the stopping of the [rebuilding of Paris] under the pretext of economy and in the hope of reducing rents. . . . The remedy of the evil does not appear to me to be the increase of liberty which would be one more weapon in hostile hands. We have seen the effect of methods of gentleness; kindness is taken for fear by men who respect nothing but force.' He urged the expulsion of industry and its workers from Paris and the continuation of the programme of destroying the old part of the city, the traditional breeding ground of revolution.[2]

The pressure for reaction became strong. 'The freedom given to spread propaganda and to form committees has benefited evil passions,' wrote Rouland, 'and the emperor sees it clearly today.' All his work for the masses has done nothing to modify their socialist tendencies. 'People are frightened in the provinces and are beginning to cast grave doubts on universal suffrage. In my opinion, a government must be faithful to its principles, and if the emperor is convinced that a strong and respected government is the

[1] Billault to Napoleon, draft, 7.7.1857, Billault papers.
[2] Haussmann to Napoleon, 8.7.1857, Billault papers.

salvation of this country, he must return to it in order to destroy the germ of the agitation.'[1]

Napoleon himself wrote to Billault: 'I think, as you do, that we must reflect seriously about the results of the last elections, but it all consists in finding the means to reduce the number of the discontented in Paris and Lyons. Only these means are difficult to find. You know how a long time ago I wanted to issue a decree or to propose a law to prevent the building of any more factories in Paris, but you also know all the objections which this proposal produced. Whenever a proposal is made in our country which is out of the ordinary, you find almost everywhere invincible aversion to it.'[2]

With the government thus alarmed, and wondering what to do, it is quite clear why the attempted assassination of Napoleon six months later, on 14 January 1858, was followed by such severe measures. That attempt was the work of an Italian and had nothing to do with the French socialists. It simply gave the opportunity for the reaction which the election had suggested.

[1] Rouland to Baroche, Baroche papers 1005, 22.7.1857.
[2] 9.7.1857, copy, Billault papers.

CHAPTER VI

*How the government won elections in its early
years and why it later ceased to win them*

THE overwhelming success of the government at the first
two general elections was no doubt due in some measure
to the state of public opinion, but public opinion is not
a spontaneous and independent force in politics, which
elections have the function of registering and converting
into numerical terms. It has to be organised and created,
and governments had sought to do this since the time of
the restoration. Now at length the system, long developed,
reached its zenith. It became rather like the system based
on the management of influence and interest, which pre-
vailed in eighteenth-century England. Though the methods
of Newcastle and Walpole might smell of corruption, they
did in fact enable the king's government to function with
greater ease than in the reign of Anne, when the queen
had failed to 'make her parliament'. So likewise did
Napoleon III's system fulfil a function.

It was based, first of all, on official candidates. The
government was simply a party in power; it must join in
the election fight like any other party, and not abstain in
the hope that M.P.s favourable to it might possibly be
returned. There was nothing radically new in this system.
The opposition claimed that formerly the government
merely recommended candidates but did not electioneer in
their favour, and the empire has therefore won a reputation
for packing its parliaments.[1] In fact it was merely its
extraordinary success which earned it its bad name for

[1] ACL 1863, 1. 86-7. Plichon.

methods which, as every reader of Balzac knows, had started long before. Villèle had, in 1822, issued a circular recommending that 'All those who are members of my ministry must, to keep their jobs, contribute within the limits of their right to the election of M.P.s sincerely attached' to the government.[1] Peyronnet, keeper of the seals, likewise proclaimed two years later that 'whoever accepts a state job contracts at the same time the obligation to devote his efforts, his talents and his influence to the service of the government'.[2] Nor was this active participation of the government a mere vice of cynical and corrupt régimes. The minister of the Interior of the idealistic second republic wrote this to his subordinates: 'Ought the government to participate in the elections or simply confine itself to ensuring their orderly conduct? I have no hesitation in replying that it would be guilty of abdication or even treason if it confined itself to making out the official returns and to counting the votes. It must enlighten France and work openly to foil the intrigues of the counter revolution.'[3]

There were men who claimed that this system would inevitably produce M.P.s who would be mere tools in the hands of the government. Tocqueville in 1837 thus refused the status of official candidate on this ground. 'I want to be in a position', he said, 'to give intelligent and independent support to the government. . . . I know very well that there are people who forget how they got into the house once they are there, but I am not one of these. I wish to reach it in the same position as I wish to keep inside it, that is, one of independence.' The prime minister of the day, Molé, replied to him and justified the system in these words: 'In my opinion my first duty is to fight in the elections as elsewhere for the opinion which brought

---

[1] S. Charlety, *La Restauration*, 183. [2] *Ibid.* 195.
[3] Circular of 8.4.1848 in Billault papers; and of 10.4.1848, F(1a*) 2097, No. 47.

me into power. . . . I do not therefore admit that to be returned through our influence would mean accepting a yoke from which delicacy or pride could suffer, or that to separate yourself from us later on a question on which you could in all conscience and conviction support us, that this would be betraying us.' Will you be freer if you are elected by legitimists, republicans or any other party? 'You must choose; isolation is not independence and you will be dependent more or less on those who elected you. The ministry's army in the elections is not composed only of men employed by it and owing their existence to it, it is composed above all of men thinking as it does and believing it good for the country that it should remain in power and that it should defeat its opponents. It is among these men, my dear sir, that I would have been happy and proud to meet you.'[1]

The first condition of success in elections was thus active participation and the principal instruments of this participation were the mayors. Through the mayors of France the government could speak to every man in the country. Each commune with one or two hundred electors had a mayor almost always invested with its confidence, but appointed by the state and having therefore all the weight of government authority behind his influence. As the state's representative he was the leader, the guide, and the indispensable aid to every man in his village. He could make life very difficult for any man who displeased him and could be very useful to his favourites. He could say to anyone who sought to go against his wishes: 'You want a road laid down to your farm — well, you won't have it. . . . You want your card signed — well, you'll have to go and get hold of the curate. . . . You will have need of me, but you won't find me.'[2]

'The mayor holds the electors in his hand', wrote a

[1] *Œuvres complètes d'Alexis de Tocqueville publiées par Madame de Tocqueville* (1866), 6. 71-5.   [2] C. 1367, I.-&-V., protest.

judge of the peace. '. . . He has daily contacts with them, it is to him that they run on the most petty business, he is their adviser and very often their conciliator; and from this is born the confidence and the deference which the electors in the communes have for their mayor, whom they look upon as a father.'[1]

The mayor was in turn most anxious that his commune should elect the official candidate unanimously, that it might testify to the sound principles he had inculcated into it and the supremacy he enjoyed over it. 'A mayor who has not enough influence over the people he administers to make them vote for the official candidate of the government', said a sub-prefect, 'ought not to hold his post.'[2] It was seldom fear of dismissal, however, which made the mayor work for the government. It was a natural desire to oblige men who could be obliging in return. Strong personal relations with the sub-prefect were frequent; the M.P. was often a very useful man to the mayor; and there were, of course, the noble mayors for whom the whole affair was a private arrangement based on almost purely personal considerations. Like Jane Austen's Mr. Dashwood, these men had a great respect for influential men and were glad to place them in their debt. One of them wrote thus to his prefect: 'I accept with great pleasure your candidate M. de Chaumont-Quitry, not because he is a chamberlain but because he is related to the emperor whom I like and admire. I know his wife's family very well; she is the daughter of the comte d'Orglandes, a neighbour of my brother-in-law, the comte de Semalé-Cromeral, who knows them very well. You do not tell me whether you know M. de Quitry personally. Has he any ability or any merit? He is very rich and that is already something. I shall see to the business of his election straight away.'[3]

[1] A.D. Haute-Garonne 2M/34, J.P., Grenade to prefect, 22.6.1857.
[2] Quoted C. 1347, Anatole Lemercier's protest, Charente-Inf.
[3] A.D. Sarthe, M61/16 bis, Baron de Gemasse to prefect.

Now under the second empire more than ever before, the prestige and power of the administration was at its zenith and the government was the concentrated source of all action; the standing of the mayor, as its representative, augmented accordingly and the government, by consciously backing him up and seeking to increase his authority, brought him, too, to the zenith of his power.[1] He had solid arguments to urge the electors to vote as he pleased. It was, first of all, in everybody's material interest to vote for the government. The essential basis of the centralisation of France is the poverty of the communes. Nominally, since they elect their own councils, they can do as they please; but in practice they cannot since they have not enough money. Their taxes go almost entirely to the state, and it is from the state, therefore, that they must beg back their money in order to carry out the thousand little improvements they most urgently need and of whose necessity they are most immediately aware.

It is essential for them to keep on good terms with the government in order to get the subsidies they require. These facts were put before the electors in plain language and were generally understood. One mayor was criticised for being too plain and thus justified himself, in a half literate style which this translation seeks to render faithfully. 'I have the honour to reply to your letter dated 30 May ult. and to certify that when I invited the electors to come and vote for M. Segris [the official candidate] I did not say that if the commune voted for him it would get whatever it wanted from you, I only engaged them to come to vote that all had a duty to fulfil this obligation which the inhabitants of Soulaines owe to be grateful for the favours we have received from the government, until this day for all our undertaking, that we need to keep the good harmony in order that we may get still more aid to finish the road works which by ourselves are unable owing to lack of

[1] F(1c) III, Ardèche 8, prefect, 12.11.1852.

finance to be completed . . .'[1]   Such motives were in
fact frequently decisive.   Here is how the judge of the
peace of Seilhac reported on the prospects in his canton
in the election of 1863.   'The commune of Beaumont will
be unanimous.   This commune has just voted for the
levying of an extraordinary rate to raise 500 francs to mend
its church ; the cost of the work is 800 francs.   It awaits a
subsidy of the remaining 300 francs from you.'   The vote
was accordingly 133 for the government and only 2 against.
'The commune of Pierrefitte will also be unanimous.   Like
the former it has voted an extraordinary rate of 4000 francs
for a parsonage.   The cost will be 6000 francs.   It is asking
you for a subsidy of 2000 francs.'   The result was 130 for,
1 against.   'It is important, *M. le Préfet*, that the grant of
these subsidies should be announced before the date of the
election. . . .   Before yesterday I visited the whole of the
commune of Chamboulive and despite all that has been
done, it will vote almost unanimously and with enthusiasm.
The change in the direction of the [proposed] road has
produced its effect.'   Result : 528 for, 71 against.[2]

The mayor was, of course, the man who understood
forms and the technical paraphernalia of bureaucratic
government, and many ignorant electors carried out the
formalities of voting in the way he told them.   The system
of voting was different to that now used in England.   The
voter was not presented with a list of candidates and asked
to place a cross against one of them.   Instead he was required to put in the box a ballot paper which he had to
produce himself, bearing the name of his favourite.   These
ballot papers were generally supplied by the candidates,
and the practice was for them to print about three times as
many ballot papers as there were electors and to distribute
them widely.   The government would send the ballot
paper of its candidate, together with a card which entitled

---

[1] A.D. Maine-et-Loire, 8M53, mayor of Soulaines to prefect, 4.6.1863.
[2] A.D. Corrèze, 62M, 25.5.1863.

a man to vote, to all electors. Every elector thus inevitably received a government ballot paper. The ignorant among them, therefore, frequently came to vote with their electoral card and their government ballot paper, which they would put in the box as though it was the only ballot paper available.

Candidates who did not visit the communes were frequently mere names. So when some poor peasant came to the village hall with a ballot paper an opposition agent had given him, the mayor presiding over the box would at once spot it.

'Ah! Haven't you got any other ballot paper apart from that one?'

'Why, yes, *M. le Maire*.'

'Show me.'

The elector shows several. The mayor takes the official candidate's and says, 'Here, my good man, this is the *good one*, put the others down——' Then the mayor puts it into the box. Or he would say, 'Put the ballot paper you've got into your pocket and take this one; this is the *good one*'.[1]

Such proceedings took place when the mayor was a paternal figure and the elector a submissive peasant. But sometimes a more arrogant man would march into the voting hall and demand a ballot paper. He is given the official candidate's. He asks for 'another one'. The mayor says there are no others. The man insists. The mayor gets angry. A row would start; and the man would probably end up by being evicted.[2] Of course, the mayor would receive great sympathy, for was not this desire to vote against his advice a challenge of his authority, a doubt cast upon his knowledge of how administrative business should be carried out? It was for personal reasons rather than because of political preferences that the mayors

[1] C. 1367, I.-&-V., Rouxin's protest.
[2] C. 1347. A. Lemercier's protest, Charente-Inf.

lost their tempers with organisers of opposition. They looked upon it as a personal insult. One mayor, no more pompous than most, thus writes to his prefect: 'Yesterday three men travelled over my commune, putting up red posters everywhere in favour of M. Casimir-Périer; when I and a gendarme asked them by what right they were putting up notices on the wall of the town hall without my authorisation, they replied in an *impertinent* manner, that they had no need of my authorisation'.[1] This was a slur on his dignity and his rage can be imagined.

The mayor was the key man in this system and it was to a great extent he who determined the results of elections. To assist him, however, he had a large body of men. 'In each commune, the official candidate has the services of ten civil servants, ten free and disciplined agents who put up his posters and distribute his ballot papers and his circulars daily; one mayor, one deputy mayor, one school-master, one constable, one road-man, one bill-sticker, one tax-collector, one postman, one licensed innkeeper, one tobacconist, appointed, approved and authorised by the prefect . . .'[2] The work of these men is best described in their own words. One schoolmaster rejoiced in 'the influence which I have the good fortune to exercise over my friends and peaceful inhabitants of Bellecombe, who never go to vote without dropping in on me to collect their ballot papers. . . . I had recourse to a little stratagem to make my (fifty two) firemen vote. I had it announced, by the beat of the drum, on Saturday evening that an inspection of arms would be held on the morrow, Sunday, after vespers; and after this inspection I made a short speech which achieved its object very well, since they all cried, "To the vote, Long live the Emperor", etc. . . .'[3] Here

[1] A.D. Isère 8M13, mayor of Valbonnais, 27.5.1863.
[2] *L'Avenir du Gers*, 5.11.1868, quoted in *La Révolution de 1848*, vol. 29, p. 171.
[3] *Instituteur* of Bellecombe to the Inspector of the Academy of Isère, 23.6.1857, A.D. Isère 8M12.

is a report of another of these schoolmasters. 'Now, *M. l'Inspecteur*, here is how I acted on this solemn occasion. As secretary of the town hall, entrusted in this capacity with the preparation of all the election documents, I was able to exercise far greater influence on the elections. In conjunction with the village constable, I distributed the ballot papers I received from *M. le Préfet* to the electors ; I strongly supported the candidature of M. Arnaud, the government's candidate. I tried to make the electors understand that we must all without exception consolidate the plans of our august emperor by a unanimous vote. Despite this, I was compelled to redouble my zeal and energy owing to the fact that some agitators had led astray a large number of electors and particularly twenty electors at a village not far away who had been earnestly solicited to vote for M. Dupont-Delporte and were completely disposed to vote for the latter and in consequence to reject the government's candidate. Having heard this vexatious news, I went to make them see the error into which they had fallen. To prove to them that the government is good, I gave them knowledge of a letter which *M. le Maire* of the commune had received from *M. le Préfet*, in which it is said that a new subsidy of 220,000 francs had just been given to the department to be divided between the communes which had suffered in the floods of 1856. In the presence of this testimony of the solicitude of the government, will you be so ungrateful, I told them, as to refuse it your co-operation : and at once they all threw down the ballot papers that had been given to them and came at once to the town hall to vote for M. Arnaud.'[1]

The zeal of some schoolmasters knew no bounds, and, that all might go well, the schoolmaster of La-Chapelle-du-Bard in Isère decorated the polling-booth with flags and exhortatory inscriptions. When the voters entered the

[1] *Instituteur* of Versoud to the inspector of the Academy of Grenoble, A.D. Isère 8M12, 23.6.1857.

room they saw a notice: 'La-Chapelle-du-Bard: Long
live the emperor'. On the right was placed a bust of His
Majesty inscribed, 'Long live the emperor. Long live the
empress. Long live the prince imperial.' On the left,
'Through the genius of its emperor, France is today the
nation which teaches all others by precept and by example'.
And finally, in front, 'Gratitude! Devotion!'[1]

The postmen likewise played their part. The illiterate
were frequently in the habit of asking them to read the
letters they delivered; the postmen were accordingly
briefed and were able to explain the meaning of the electoral propaganda they delivered on behalf of the government.[2] The bill-sticker was delegated not only to put up
the election posters, but also to watch over their staying
up and to replace them at once if they were torn down.[3]

The activities of all these men were co-ordinated by
their superiors. The judges of the peace would tour their
cantons, talk to the mayors and the notables of each village
and report on them. The inspector of primary education,
on the basis of information from the village schoolmasters,
sent daily reports on the attitude of mayors, clergy and
communes in general. The government thus knew where
it was weak. An energetic prefect might accordingly write
five hundred personal letters to inflame the zeal of influential men who might help in dangerous areas.[4] The prefect
was responsible for the whole operation and would 'answer
for its success' to the minister. The sub-prefect likewise
regarded it as a personal matter to win; and a victory in an
election of exceptional difficulty would gain him promotion.

The elections were decided by the individual votes of
individual people, each with their own reasons for the
actions they took. In every village it was known perfectly

---

[1] A.D. Isère 8M13, mayor of La-Chapelle-du-Bard to prefect, 3.6.1863.
[2] A.D. Aveyron, 1863 election file, mayor of Montbazens to prefect.
[3] A.D. Isère 8M13, notes of expenditure, Morel, *afficheur à Grenoble*.
[4] Chevreau to Billault, 2.6.1863, Billault papers. A.D. Maine-et-Loire
8M51.

well how each man voted just as it very often still is today. Every villager knows who the communists are, so likewise everybody knew who the rioters of December 1851 had been, or who were the priest's devotees or the henchmen of the local count. In theory the government knew how every elector in the country was disposed to it, and it therefore generally knew the results of the elections fairly accurately in advance.

One of the main reasons for the government's success in its first ten years was that the mayors' authority was so great that they were able to influence the doubtful to vote the right way and to organise the faithful to come and register their votes. It was not infrequent, of course, for the mayor to be either incompetent or hostile and for the government to be unable to find anyone else able or willing to replace him. Thus in the west the local legitimist noble was very often kept as mayor of his village. Sometimes this was the case because there was not a single man it could substitute, and the government was dependent on his good-will. Sometimes it was because the noble was anxious to continue to bolster his influence with the added prestige of a government agent and he would offer to co-operate with the prefect, to be a useful though uncertain ally. In some cases, however, the prefect would find some able, well-to-do peasant to become mayor, who with the backing of the government would build up a strong position and drive the noble into utter isolation and impotence in his château. That was how the government made conquests and increased its following. Yet this shows also how the government had weak mayors in the very areas where it was weak in any case.

Now what chance had the opposition against such a system? What could they offer which the government could not? They could, of course, offer far more, as oppositions always do. There was a man who must have stood in well over a hundred constituencies in the elections of this period : he fulfilled the legal conditions and distributed his propaganda, though he seldom got more than five votes anywhere. His 'profession of faith', however, is worth quoting because it is unwittingly an excellent parody, carried to farcical exaggeration, of the majority of opposition circulars.

'Electors, If I am elected, aided and supported by you, I will be able to tell and to teach all the sovereigns and all the world what is needed to prevent all human miseries and to establish at once and for ever universal peace on eternal foundations.

'I come today to ask you for a mandate of confidence, basing my demand on the wide knowledge I have acquired by my observations in my travels and by my lifelong studies, theoretical and practical, in agriculture, industry, trade, law administration, finance etc. etc., and on the strength of my conscience, for I know that not a word can be said against my private life, nor against my public life ; I come, I say, to ask you for a mandate to represent you as M.P. and above all to become and really be, one day in the very near future, the first legislator of the Human Race — a job which no one has yet filled — a job, you may be certain, which I shall know how to fill worthily, that is as a true and good Frenchman, as a really humane man.

'My election will mark the advent of perfection in all and everywhere. What constituency therefore will elect me, to be by that the initiator of a perfect world ? Know, gentlemen, that I am completely ready to carry out this work, awaited for so long and so earnestly desired.

ADOLPHE BERTRON,
Humane Candidate.

Signed in Sceaux (Seine), the Little Park and the Little Palace of Humanity.'[1]

The promises of the opposition in general might be made with more caution, though quite frequently without

[1] A.D. Maine-et-Loire 8M51.

more modesty. The comte de Chambrun distributed an album of engravings to enable all illiterate peasants to appreciate his value, depicting various episodes in his glorious and beneficent career. It showed him repressing a demagogic insurrection in December 1851 as prefect of Jura ; then Louis Napoleon is seen at his desk writing to congratulate him, and the congratulation is recited. Now he is helping the sick in the cholera epidemic ; now he is gravely taking part in a meeting of a parliamentary committee ; now he is speaking before the council of state and by his skill obtaining the first railway for his department. Scenes of rejoicing in various towns make manifest the pleasure with which he is everywhere greeted. And his wife is no less addicted to the public good ; she accompanies him incessantly on their perpetual visits to all parts of the department. She visits the poor and the sick and she places gifts in churches.[1]

These heights of illustrated propaganda were, however, not attempted by the majority of the opposition candidates. They confined themselves to pointing out that though they might be undistinguished, they were essentially well meaning : they promised higher wages and lower prices, economy and less taxation but also more roads, railways and subsidies for their own constituency ; liberty and peace and glory.

Promises were of no avail if they were not distributed and explained to individual voters, and for this there were plenty of agents to hand. Almost every commune had its quota of discontented men, rivals or personal enemies of the mayor, old reds of the republic. It needed only one man in a commune to write out a few hundred ballot papers for the opposition candidate, and to distribute them to whoever he thought suitable. In one commune, for example, forty-two votes were cast against the government in 1869. This, says the local judge of the peace, was due

[1] B.N. Ln(27) 3836.

to the deputy mayor who had been dissatisfied ever since someone else had been made mayor instead of him; he had allied with the dismissed doctor of the canton, and together they had raised this vote.[1] Great landowners might similarly canvass all the men with whom they had relations, and in some areas they could exercise their influence through religious and charitable societies as well.[2] Energetic candidates would tour their constituencies, talk to as many men as they could, and leave their propaganda and ballot papers with suitable people. Those among them who were industrialists would use their workers to do the canvassing for them. The opposition, therefore, did not have the system or the organisation of the government and it was, as a result, inevitably sporadic and scattered.

It was not so, however, in the towns. Here the government did indeed have a mayor, but one who had a hundred times as many men to look after and who therefore had little to do with them individually. The government had, as Prince Napoleon said, no 'means of exerting pressure' in the towns,[3] and the towns thus were ideal breeding grounds for organised opposition. In the clubs, in the cafés, where old conspirators could capture men without the ties of the country, in the workshops where radicalism was frequently an occupational habit, among the dregs of the unemployed, and among the bourgeoisie recently evicted from their positions of influence — from such sources both officers and armies could be recruited.

After 1860 there are signs of a new spirit in some elections. Villages which had till then followed their mayors united to the polls, do so no longer, and by 1869 there are few communes which register unanimous votes.

[1] A.D. Haute-Garonne 2M36, J.P., Cadours to prefect, 25.5.1869.
[2] *E.g.* F(1c) III, Hérault 9, minister of Interior to prefect, draft, 23.10.1858; F(1c) II 103, Vaucluse file.
[3] Jerome-Napoleon to Napoleon, E. d'Hauterive, *Napoléon III et le prince Napoléon*, 386-95.

Why was this so? The development of public opinion had a great deal to do with it, of course, but no less important was the decay of the system of managing elections as a whole. The government was weak where the mayors were weak. 'The places where we cannot bring our influence to bear', wrote a sub-prefect in 1863, 'are nearly always those where the mayor is not in perfect harmony with his municipal council. The good organisation of the municipalities is today the corner-stone of the governmental structure.'[1] The reason for the lack of harmony and the reason for the weakness of the mayors is to be found in the policy of the government itself.

First, it vacillated and yielded before the attacks the system received. In 1860 Billault had decided to appoint the mayors before the local elections and to invite them not to stand as candidates. In this way, he claimed, they would be in a stronger position to dominate the rivalries of the communes. They would be purely and simply the representatives of the executive and could thus exert an independent and impartial control.[2] This move was designed to strengthen them but it had one cardinal vice, that the mayors, the government's most important agents for the management of universal suffrage, were to have their connection with universal suffrage severed and to declare themselves doubtful of its confidence in them. In fact, two-thirds of the mayors ignored the minister's instructions and presented themselves for election: only about a tenth of them were defeated. The consequent disarray was aggravated by the government's reversing its policy at the next local election. It declared that it would appoint the mayors only after the elections, from the elected members of the municipal councils; which was, of course, a complete abdication to the demands of the opposition.[3]

[1] A.D. Isère 8M13, sub-prefect, Latour-du-Pin, to prefect, 5.6.1863.
[2] M.U. 6. and 10.81.860.
[3] A.N. 45 AP 1, note by Rouher to Napoleon, probably 1864.

Secondly, the government ceased to give the mayors the backing which had been the basis of their influence. Then, worst of all, the concession of the right to hold meetings enabled the opposition to set up committees in every commune. Hence, exactly when the government's electoral agents were being thrown into confusion, the opposition's were given the opportunity to organise.[1]

The opposition had indeed by now learnt how important the mayors were; they began to chase around their constituencies, trying to win their support and seeking to be declared the mayor's candidates. Renegade mayors who deserted to the opposition ceased to be uncommon; and, moreover, the government seldom dismissed them when they did desert. Here is the report of a judge of the peace which shows the sort of thing that began to happen. 'Yesterday I was at the town of Lagraulière. I examined it and was surprised that *M. le Maire* had not had the official candidature of M. Mathieu posted up, even though I had given instructions to the deputy mayor about this. I spoke to him again; he replied that *M. le Maire* had the posters at his house. Not a single one has been put up. . . . Yesterday morning *M. le Maire* had announced in the market place the candidature of M. Mathieu very briefly and in one single sentence, saying he was put up by the government; and he announced loudly the candidature of M. de Jouvenel [the opposition candidate], thrice repeating that he had on three successive occasions been elected M.P. by the people. I do not know whether he has the right to do this. I was assured that all his family was active, even his wife, and that they were giving money for drinks [in favour of the opposition]. . . .' The result was that the government only scraped a bare majority in this commune.[2]

---

[1] Persigny to Napoleon, draft, 27.7.1865. B.N.N.A.Fr. 23066 f. 331.
[2] A.D. Corrèze 62M, J.P., Seilhac, 25.5.1863.

While the government's electoral army was disintegrating, the opposition was busy building armies of its own. There was a mayor in every commune, but also a priest and a schoolmaster. The candidates who opposed Napoleon's papal and ecclesiastical policy often found an admirable force for canvassing the electorate in the clergy who could use the pulpit, the confessional and the women, and who did not hesitate to visit all their parishioners in their homes.[1] Schoolmasters were often won by the republicans. Local committees became common once again. The opposition discovered a weak point in the electoral law of 1852. It had been decreed that in order to be elected, a candidate must obtain the votes of at least a quarter of the electorate and more than half the votes actually cast. If this condition was not fulfilled, a second vote was necessary, when the man who got the most votes won. Now the opposition began putting up as many candidates as possible, of whatever shade of opinion, in the hope of collecting enough votes, not to get one of their candidates in, but to prevent the government's candidate obtaining the minimum necessary number of votes. If they succeeded, a second ballot was held at which the opposition united all their votes on that candidate who stood most chance of winning.[2]

The opposition began to use the press to greater effect. Now the press was regarded as one of the most powerful means of propaganda and as an essential basis for a candidate standing for parliament. Successive régimes had all recognised its power and had created newspapers 'to enlighten the inhabitants of the countryside on their real interests, by putting before their eyes now the grievous results which the spirit of rebellion produces, now examples of devotion and of loyalty given by the best citizens'.[3] But they consistently failed to capture the Paris papers with

[1] *E.g.* A.D. Loire-Inf. 1 M 100/3, report of sub-prefect, St-Nazaire.
[2] É. Ollivier, *L'Empire libéral*, 3. 3-14.   Article 6, decree of 2.2.1852.
[3] *Journal de la Côte-d'Or*, quoted by S. Fizaine, *La Vie politique dans la Côte-d'Or sous Louis XVIII*, 87.

huge circulations; and their own papers were always in a small minority. In 1861, for example, the government had three main papers and two very minor ones with a total circulation of 52,832. Even if the *Journal officiel's* 17,242 is added to this figure, it remains much below that of the 'progressive' papers' total of 91,292, the Orleanists' 36,859 and the legitimists' and clericals' 38,285.[1] The government inevitably had to rely on its censorship and even more on the threat of prohibition to keep these papers from being too hostile. It was helped by the fact that they were nearly always as much great financial speculations as political weapons devoted to a cause. By 1869, however, the new press law let loose the hostility of the great papers and allowed them to distribute a daily vilification of the government to hundreds of thousands of readers.

However, the effect of this press law was even more important in the departments. Here the government was far stronger than the opposition. In 1862 the distribution of the provincial press was this:

The government had 202 papers with 207,071 subscribers.
The Orleanists had   13 papers with   20,069 subscribers.
The legitimists had 34 papers with   31,134 subscribers.
The republicans had 13 papers with   22,981 subscribers.[2]

As many as half the departments had no opposition paper at all. The *coup d'état* had been followed by a massacre of the provincial press and most of the republican papers had disappeared.[3] It was, indeed, difficult for a local paper to survive independently. It could not hope for much income from advertisements, since the prefect's paper was normally given a monopoly of the legal ones which were the most valuable. The local papers were nearly always run at a loss and even those of the government were subsidised from central funds alone to an extent of 114,275 francs.[4]

[1] F(18) 294.   [2] F(18) 294.
[3] Maupas' report on the press, copy, 3.2.1853, A.N., ABXIX 175.
[4] F(18) 307; note by director-general; 1868 figure.

Opposition candidates considered a local paper essential to success. What they produced was in fact a newspaper only in name: it was generally merely political polemic casting accusations on the government and replying to accusations against itself. It was very frequently distributed free of charge in huge quantities and accordingly cost a great deal of money. The expenses might be borne by a rich candidate alone, or by a group of friends prepared to pay for success. Now, between the press law of 1868 and the elections of 1869, about 150 new papers appeared in the provinces, 120 of which were hostile, and in ten departments the opposition found itself with more subscribers than the government. These new papers represented an outlay of two million francs, which shows how powerful was the opposition's participation in politics.[1]

Money indeed was coming to play an increasing part in politics, and this is the final reason for the disintegration of the government's system. The government had at its disposal the innumerable subsidies, grants and concessions which it was its job to make, but which it could store up to use for electoral purposes. It spent very little extra money on elections, for the only considerable item on the account at the end of each one was that for printing circulars and ballot papers. The former cost about ten francs a hundred, the latter three francs a hundred; the cost for each constituency would therefore be around a thousand francs; and sometimes the candidates would pay this themselves.[2] The government's great advantage was that it had to pay only the printers and that all other services were performed free of charge, apart from small tips, by the civil service. The presents the official candidates made to charities, to churches and to schools were not of great importance.[3]

---

[1] F(18) 307, director-general's note, and summary of provincial press.
[2] A.D. Haute-Garonne 2M36 ; A.D. Isère 8M13 ; A.D. Nord M 30/11, 9.9.1863.
[3] *E.g.* BB(30) 427, *procureur général*, Bordeaux, 18.5.1863.

Now, however, there begins to appear a new type of candidate, who virtually bought himself a seat, since it was money which played the predominant part in his election. The classic case is that of Bravay, a merchant who had made a huge fortune in Egypt, and who had returned to his native Gard to find a severe shortage of water and the long-prepared plans for a canal from the Rhône to remedy it still fruitless. He announced with a great fanfare of publicity that he would build it. He held a stupendous opening ceremony at which the spectators were given free refreshments, and thus having made himself into the local hero and benefactor, he stood for parliament and was elected. The point of this story is made all the more striking by the fact that, though vast sums of money were spent on entertainment and publicity, the shares of the canal company which he established were not in fact sold and the land for it not even bought. Twice was his election invalidated, but twice was he none the less re-elected.[1]

Similarly Daniel Wilson, a young man of 29, son of a Scotsman who had made his fortune by introducing gas lighting to Paris, gave lavish entertainments at his country house, to which he brought voters in his carriages ; and he was duly elected. Laroche-Joubert, a great paper manufacturer of Angoulême, is said to have spent a hundred thousand francs on his election and to have sent five hundred of his workers to canvass for him. He was returned unopposed at the general election the following year because no one felt disposed to go to the expense of challenging him.[2]

These are outstanding instances in a general tendency to use drink and money and impossible promises to win seats. It was an introduction, men said, of English electioneering methods into French life : men had become

---

[1] C. 1349. ACL 1864, 1. 179-99, ACL 1865, 2. 4-6.
[2] C. 1367, Indre-et-Loire. BB(30) 427, *procureur général*, Bordeaux, 23.11.1868. BB(18) 1786, *idem*, 31.5.1869.

cynical and said they would get into parliament even if it cost them one or two hundred thousand francs. The electors were becoming more and more spoilt and their demands were increasing.[1] Quite apart from the purely corrupt aspect of this movement, the government found the opposition playing its own game against it. The mayor of a small commune in the eastern Pyrenees tells how he was offered a thousand francs for his village if he would vote for a particular candidate. He refused, he said, but he could have done with the money. They had some good fountains half a mile away but could not afford the pipes to bring the water to the village. The church was in need of repair and there was still half a mile of the road to the local capital to be constructed. Every commune had pressing needs such as these, and any wealthy man would be a god-send, whatever his politics. In this case it was Pereire who was the millionaire they picked upon.[2]

It was in such ways that the business of electioneering became more complicated and more difficult for the government. Universal suffrage, wrote Chevreau to Billault in 1862, 'is beginning to tell us that it is no longer willing to be guided [*conduit*]; and if we are not all very clever and light-handed, we shall, I believe, have many disappointments at the general elections'.[3] The government's problem could be solved by skill, as some demanded. Or it could be solved by resignation and by withdrawing from the elections in the way the liberal empire did. Yet the system of official candidates had its use and served a purpose in the development of French institutions. It disciplined the electorate and thus enabled universal suffrage to be practised without violence and to become ingrained in the habits of the nation. In the early years of

---

[1] ACL 1869, 2. 50, J. David's interpellation on bribery ; BB(30) 427. *procureur général*, Bordeaux, 18.6.1863 ; BB(30) 429, *procureur général*, Douai, 17.6.1863 ; Brochant de Villers to Baroche, Bibl. Thiers 987 f. 198, 12.12.1858.

[2] ACL 1864, 1. 315-16.   [3] 5.8.1862, Billault papers.

the empire men could still talk of abolishing it as being too dangerous. After Napoleon there could be no serious question of any such move. Such is the place which the second empire's system of 'packing' holds in the history of France.

CHAPTER VII

Why liberal concessions were made in 1860[1]

A LIBERAL M.P. who had protested against the *coup d'état* and withdrawn from politics recalled many years later a story which illustrates the state of public opinion in 1852. 'When I had returned to the Vosges after the *coup d'état*, I received a visit from a well-to-do peasant who lived in a neighbouring commune.

'"Ah, well," said he, "here you are, you have broken with Napoleon."

'"I think," said I, "that it is Napoleon who has broken with me."

'"How's that?"

'"You had given me a mandate; was it not my duty to defend it?"

'"Yes, certainly, your conduct is very honourable and no-one can reproach you. But we, sir, we have no mandate."

'"No, without doubt, since you are the electors who give the mandate."

'"Well, sir, I shall speak to you in all sincerity. The commune I inhabit is excellent; it is composed of an immense majority of good chaps, very attached to good order, to peace and calm. We have, however, got four or

---

[1] *Decree of 24 November 1860*: 'Napoleon, etc., wishing to give the great bodies of the state a more direct part in the formation of the general policy of our government and a striking testimony of our confidence in them, have decreed and decree . . .' that the debates of the two houses should be published in full, that they should vote an address to the throne every year, that the government would appoint ministers without portfolio to represent it in parliament, and that, 'in order to facilitate the expression of the legislature's opinion in the making of laws', its powers of amending them be increased.

five stubborn fellows and one or two fools, capable of very bad deeds if circumstances allow them to count on impunity. Six months ago, if, while crossing my village, where I am regarded, although mistakenly, as the richest inhabitant, I met one of these daring fellows, he would look at me in a menacing way and I would sometimes even hear him murmur: *Wait, wait till 1852. The rich. You'll see——*. [The triumph of the reds was expected in 1852.] Upon my faith, sir, I confess I was neither proud nor felt reassured. Today I cross my village holding my head high. I look these chaps straight in the face. People say we have lost all our liberties. As for me, I avow it, I am only beginning to find myself free." [1]

In such conditions there was no question of re-establishing parliamentary government, yet the extraordinary thing is that the liberal empire had its roots in the very beginnings of the régime. 'After the *coup d'état*,' wrote Rouher, who took a leading part in drawing up the constitution of 1852, 'everybody thought it impossible not to take into account the new political habits which the country had acquired in the preceding fifty years. The legislature was given the right of discussion. Now its power was in germ in this provision. Its whole development was merely a question of time.' [2]

The second empire thus did not seek merely to re-establish the institutions of the first one. Napoleon III publicly declared that his government was to be authoritarian only for a time. It was his proud boast that he, alone among the rivals for the throne of France, knew the need to move with the times. 'March at the head of the ideas of your century,' he declared, 'and these ideas follow you and support you. March behind them, and they drag you after them. March against them, and they overthrow you.' He stressed, therefore, that he was seeking to

---

[1] Buffet to Ollivier, Ollivier papers, 10.4.1896.
[2] A.N. 45 A.P. 2. 'Note pour l'empereur', probably of 1864.

lay foundations capable of supporting the development of liberty in the future. 'A constitution', he quoted his uncle as saying, 'is the work of time ; one cannot leave too large an opening for ameliorations', and he accordingly included provisions in it for its improvement by constitutional means. In this way he would enable France to make political progress without revolution. 'To those', he declared in 1853, 'who might regret that larger concessions had not been made to liberty, I would answer: Liberty has never helped to found a lasting political edifice ; it crowns the edifice when time has consolidated it.'[1]

This last phrase was seized upon by many politicians who frequently expressed the hope that the 'crowning of the edifice' would soon take place. An important characteristic of the constitution, they pointed out, was its elasticity which would allow the legislature to assume an increasingly influential part in it. For though in 1851 Napoleon, victorious from the plebiscite, represented the will of the nation, he would do so much less in a few years' time, and the legislature, since it was frequently re-elected, would come to represent it much better. The growing authority which it would thus inevitably acquire must result in a change in the balance of the constitution.[2]

Napoleon could hardly increase his power beyond its position in 1852 ; but the legislature could and its influence was felt more and more as it became a normal organ in the machinery of law-making. At first it was consulted rather as a matter of form, but inevitably disagreements arose and members began to ask for increased powers of amending legislation. More particularly in finance the government was regularly censured for excessive expenditure by the most devoted members, who demanded closer control in

---

[1] *Discours, messages et proclamations de l'empereur* (Plon, 1860), 202, 212 ; PVCL 1853, 1. 3. *Œuvres de Napoléon III*, 1. 342.

[2] PVCL 1852, 2. 83 and 107 ; M.U. 1853, 554-5 ; CRCL 1854, 86 ; CRCL 1855, 207 and 316-17 ; CRCL 1856, 139-40 ; CRCL 1858, 382 ; CRCL 1860, 328.

the form of the right to vote the budget in individual chapters rather than in ministries.[1] With the economic crisis of 1857, moreover, the co-operation of the legislature became more than ever necessary to the government. Money became scarce and the great public works of the time, the railways, could therefore no longer be financed by the old method of private borrowing. State aid was given to the companies and this involved the control by parliament of a matter formerly independent of it.[2]

The ministers themselves discovered that the separation of legislative and executive was inconvenient since it closed the doors of the legislature to them and left the defence of the government there to mere civil servants, the counsellors of state. Rouland found these counsellors of state unsatisfactory interpreters of his budget and twice arranged to meet the parliamentary budget commission 'by accident', for the purpose of discussing it 'as friends'.[3] Morny likewise formed the opinion that parliamentary procedure must be reformed for the improved conduct of affairs. It was absurd, he argued, that a body which was thought worth consulting should be so restricted in its powers to reform measures which it saw to be defective, and that it should be left with the alternative of rejecting them completely or allowing them to pass in an unsatisfactory state. 'Speaking in my own name', he declared to the house, 'and engaging neither the government nor anyone else, I also think something needs to be done about it.' He began working on a revision of the rules of parliamentary procedure and privately asked the five opposition members not to attack the existing procedure any more, so that he could reform it without appearing to yield to them.[4] Finally, the Italian

---

[1] PVCL 1860, 6. 787 and 1294-6 ; CRCL 1859, 372 and 374 ; CRCL 1854, 442, 448, 463 ; CRCL 1855, 559-60, 585 ; CRCL 1856, 695-6, 706 ; PVCL 1858, 5. 593-6, 5. 701-3 ; PVCL 1859, 5. 414.

[2] L. Girard, *La Politique des travaux publics du second empire*, 196-208.

[3] Richemont to Persigny, 8.6.1860, Persigny papers.

[4] PVCL 1860, 6. 1294-6. Ollivier's diary, 7.7.1860.

war and the free trade treaty had raised issues which had produced lively debates in both houses. The government had seen that their publication would help it in the defence of its own policy and it had accordingly published the proceedings of the senate.

Meanwhile other pressures were exerting their influence. The novelty of the concessions of 24 November 1860 has thrown into the shade the ministerial changes which accompanied them. The position of Achille Fould in the history of the second empire, though ill defined and obscure, was of the highest importance. During its first eight years he was minister of State, in which capacity he was the 'first confidant of the initiative of the emperor [and] also his most important auxiliary'. 'There is now', wrote Persigny, 'only one minister, or rather . . . there is a first minister who sums up the whole government in his person.' 'The emperor is in the hands of Fould who proposes and arranges everything.'[1] The year 1860 marked the victory of Persigny, Walewski, Haussmann and Morny against Fould, and, which was even more important, the abolition of his office. The ministry of State was now divided from the ministry of the Imperial Household and its particularly close link with the crown in this way destroyed. Fould's fall shows that the innovations of 24 November 1860 marked a radical change in system. They were also to be the inauguration of a new era, in which the emperor, having won all the military laurels he required, having presided over the congress of Europe and having augmented his territory with three departments, would devote his energy to a huge programme for the development of the national wealth.

There can be little doubt that for all the pressures exerted on Napoleon and all the intrigues of this crisis, it

[1] Senator La Guéronnière in A. Fould, *Journaux et discours*, 1867, Ln(27) 23737. Persigny to Napoleon, draft, Sept. 1854, and Persigny to his wife, 26.8.1859, Persigny papers.

was he alone who made the decision. He had left his ministers very much in the dark and in all probability he presented his proposal to the council of ministers all of a sudden. Almost certainly the idea of establishing an address to the throne was his own.[1] Experience had shown him the need for publicity and control in matters all of whose detail he could not be master. One day, probably at about this time, Napoleon was talking to the duc de Plaisance about his days as president of the republic. 'Ah! those were the days.' Plaisance said things did not seem to have worsened for him. 'You are quite wrong, my dear duke,' said Napoleon. 'At that time it was all life and movement around me; today it is silence. I am isolated, I no longer hear anything.' That a desire to free himself from the dangers of court intrigue was a dominant motive in his decision is confirmed by his own statement to the council of ministers in 1861 when he adopted Fould's financial programme, which was the completion of the series of reforms started by the amnesty and the free trade treaty. 'The emperor,' wrote Baroche, 'explaining the reasons which led him to accept M. Fould's proposals, said, "I am certainly far from admitting that our finances are in the almost desperate situation which the foreign papers suggest. We are, compared to any of the European powers, in an excellent position. It is therefore not a cry [?] of distress that I want to utter. But I could not fail to acknowledge that the impulse to spend money on useful things is strong and easy to succumb to. So I wanted to place a barrier against my ministers and against myself which would not be crossed without some previous reflection. I also wanted to destroy this notion which they pretend to hold abroad that my government is so absolute that I hold all the wealth of France in my

---

[1] Billault to Napoleon, draft, 22.11.1860, Billault papers. Morny to Napoleon, copy, 24.12.1863, in a MSS. biography of Morny by M. Quatrelles L'Épine.

hands, and that I can dispose of it as I please even for my personal needs. . . . This is one of the main causes of the fear and the suspicion which France causes abroad, because it is believed that suddenly, without any previous discussion, and hence without any publicity, I can secretly acquire huge sums, for example to make military preparations. I wanted all the world to know that this was impossible" . . .'[1]

The theory that Napoleon was merely yielding in his weakness before the attacks of the opposition was invented by that opposition to flatter its own importance. Napoleon put his ministers in parliament because he felt this would strengthen his government's position, and not because it was an opposition demand. Thiers interpreted the move intelligently when he wrote, 'The emperor's motives are these. First, it was impossible to continue the contrast of France giving liberty to all the world and refusing it for herself; and secondly, the legislature no longer worked properly with the system as it was.' He explained his interpretation more fully to the duc d'Aumale: 'The first reason for it was the state of the legislature. I think I told your highness several years ago that the *Corps de l'État* [the senate, the council of state and the legislature] could not work for long organised as they were. For when you have recourse to assemblies, you must have recourse to the methods of managing them, or otherwise it is best to do without them if you can, which I think is impossible. Now experience proves that the only means of managing them is to give the conduct of affairs to men who have their confidence or whom they merely like. Otherwise it is impossible. But to think that by sending them a poor little counsellor of state, knowing nothing, replying to nothing and giving the houses the sort of report a civil servant makes to his minister, you will manage to dominate them,

---

[1] Note by Baroche, in his papers 1035 f. 29-32 of meeting of council of ministers at Compiègne, 22.11.1861.

is a pure and puerile illusion. Such a régime is possible while the fear of the reds is supreme, but all fear comes to an end, and then the indocility characteristic of the century and of France reappears. This is what began to happen last year and M. Baroche said to anyone who cared to hear, that it was impossible to go on like that. Hence the need to *do something*. So the emperor followed partly his own inclinations and partly the way things pointed. His personal inclination has always been to think (he often used to tell me so) that repression was by nature temporary; he realised that sooner or later he would have to yield a little to the reawakening independence of opinion and he found it gave him the appearance of great wisdom to forestall the day when concessions would no longer be voluntary. I think also that his very strong affection for his son played its part in deciding him. Obviously he wanted to prepare the future for this child. As for the way things pointed, it had become striking; for to preach liberty, sword in hand, to the whole world, to tell the Pope, the king of Naples, the dukes of Tuscany and Modena, and the emperor of Austria himself, that they were perishing or would perish for having refused sufficient liberty to their subjects, and to make us live under the institutions of the first empire and of the early part of it, too, without even the corrective of the Additional Act, this had become an intolerable contrast and almost ludicrous . . .'[1]

Buffet likewise recognised that Napoleon had made a concession long before it was necessary. 'When for nine years', he wrote, 'one has seen liberal ideas discussed and ridiculed by the immense majority of the country; when one has seen, as I have in the provinces, public opinion crumble up more and more and become little by little stranger to the most simple notions of liberty, it is difficult not to rejoice with some enthusiasm at this unexpected

---

[1] Thiers to Buffet, 1.12.1860, Buffet papers. Thiers to duc d'Aumale, 6.1.1861, copy, B.N.N.A.Fr. 20618 f. 595-7.

return to the principles which are dear to us. . . . It is perhaps a unique opportunity to bring governors and governed in France together, possibly for ever, in the serious exercise of political liberty . . . and it has become possible, thanks to the happy inspiration of the emperor.'[1]

It can now be seen that the concessions of 1860 were a positive measure inspired by constructive policy and not by fear. This does not mean that its actual effects were in fact accurately foreseen by the emperor. The reactions to it were indeed diverse. The comte de Chambord insisted that his legitimist followers should continue to abstain from politics and that they should not alter their past attitude.[2] The duc d'Aumale was of course more opportunist and pliant, and his advice to a friend was made public for all Orleanists to know. 'Do not think', he wrote, 'that I attach no importance to the concessions which the imperial government has just made to liberal opinion. I doubt their sincerity and I am convinced that they contain an ulterior motive, but they certainly have their value. I am of the opinion that they should be used as much as possible, that they should even be praised as a first step which holds out hopes and which allows men to demand further concessions. We shall see how they are carried out in practice and what happens.'[3]

The opinions of these leaders, condemned to the inevitable ignorance and misinformation of exiles, do not represent accurately the reactions of their followers. The legitimists, though they professed a mystical veneration for their king and in theory felt an obligation to obey his commands, were remarkably independent in practice. It is frequently the tragedy of royalists that they are at loggerheads with their king almost as much as with their opponents. For all the king might say, at least twenty-five

---

[1] Buffet to Thiers, B.N.N.A.Fr. 20618 f. 514-16, 30.11.1860.
[2] Falloux, *Mémoires d'un royaliste*, 2. 364.
[3] Quoted by P. Guiral, *Prévost-Paradol*, 262.

legitimists stood for parliament in 1863, a number which excludes some sixteen clericals often of the same hue. The Orleanists, on the other hand, were of course essentially opportunists and followers of their party from reason rather than from sentiment. They found that if Napoleon was turning liberal, they must play the game, and accept him, since their avowed devotion was to principles and not to persons. The tone of their reaction was set by Prévost-Paradol in an article in the *Journal des Débats* where he asked, 'Are we honest men? In our incessant repetitions that we place the increase of our liberties above all else and that we demand above all the government of the nation by the nation, have we been merely play-acting?'[1] If we are honest, and if we have not been play-acting these last nine years, wrote Buffet, we must 'accept these important rights in good faith and use them fairly. If the concession is not complete, it cannot be denied that it covers what is most essential. . . . I ardently wish that we use these rights which have been restored to us, but I desire no less ardently that we do not abuse them and that by their moderation, prudence and the dignity of their conduct, the liberals should make the nation understand these constitutional guarantees which have, since 1852, been forsaken by public opinion even more than by the government.'[2]

Thiers thought the same, though he was more guarded. 'It is impossible for the liberal monarchical party which has always demanded liberty to refuse any grant of it when it is offered. What matters is not the sincerity of the offer, but the sincerity of its acceptance. We must discuss, since we are called upon to do so, the affairs of the state; discuss them sensibly and in good faith; we must put away all malice directed against the reigning dynasty and discuss business as business, with arguments drawn from business alone, and in a word, act as we did in the first

---

[1] Quoted *ibid.* 259.
[2] Buffet to Thiers, B.N.N.A.Fr. 20618 f. 514-16, 30.11.1860.

year of the revolution of 1848, when we could do some real good. On this condition we shall have the ear of the country and we shall put the government in the wrong, if it goes wrong. Any other conduct will be unwise, dishonest, and inaction would be better though it would be fatal sooner or later. Now I have not spoken of individuals. For them it is less simple to know what to do. Those who are young and new to politics, can have no objection to entering at once into action. But will they suffice for the task ? I do not think so, not because of their want of talent, but because of their want of authority and of experience. I foresee deplorable mistakes even with good leadership, and what will it be like without it ? This would lead to the conclusion that men who have acquired a name and the habit of acting themselves and leading others, should intervene. But here everything becomes difficult, because the question of dignity is immense. Even putting aside the taste for rest which has become very powerful with me, we must not forget where this road will lead. If the government resists, when it sees that liberty will challenge a part of its omnipotence, a revolution will follow and it is disagreeable for those who have been in three revolutions to take part in a fourth. If the government yields with prudence, we are quite simply its prisoners and in good faith we must agree, not to become its ministers, but to be its applauders.'[1]

[1] Thiers to duc d'Aumale, copy, 6.1.1861, B.N.N.A.Fr. 20618 f. 595-598. Cf. Thiers to Buffet, 1.12.1860, Buffet papers.

CHAPTER VIII

*How Persigny sought to meet the challenge of
the left*

(1863)

IT was Persigny's boast that after Napoleon III himself he
was the man who had done most to establish the second
empire; [1] and there is a great deal of truth in his claim.
In 1852 he had played a leading part in laying the foundations of the Bonapartist party. Now, once again minister
of the Interior, he had the opportunity of welding that
vague coalition into something more united and organic.
His role was important above all because he had a definite
policy and clear ideas on his aims and his methods. The
Bonapartes must be established in France, as firmly as the
Hanoverians had been in England, and for this the dynastic
question must cease to be a matter of debate. It was no
good hoping that the people would vote for Napoleon; a
party had to be created positively to support him. Elections therefore were not occasions on which the people
registered their preference for various theories or men, but
battles to annihilate the enemy and to weld together the
victors with the experience and the memory of the fight.

Now the previous elections had shown where Napoleon's weakness lay. 'Long before the elections', wrote
Persigny in 1865, 'I told your majesty that in the business
of elections, there were two distinct things to consider;
the provincial elections, properly so called, and those of
the great centres of population. That so far as the

---

[1] Persigny to Napoleon, 21.11.1859, draft, B.N.N.A.Fr. 23066 f. 145-6.

provinces were concerned, by appealing to the Napoleonic sentiment, by giving clear and precise instructions, by covering all the agents of the administration with my responsibility, instead of hiding mine behind theirs, I would answer for the elections there. . . . But as for the large centres of population, I told and I repeat to your majesty, that whatever the attitude of the popular masses, they escape the attraction of the government by the very nature of our administrative organisation. For, whereas in the provinces the government has an electoral agent in the mayor for every group of about a hundred electors, in the large centres of the population, it has only one mayor through whom to exert its action on twenty to thirty-five thousand electors. In other words, whereas in a provincial constituency the government counts on several [?] hundred electoral agents, that is to say, as many mayors as there are little communes and all of them in continual relations with the electors, all known, honoured and respected ; — in the constituency of a large city there is but one sole electoral agent, but one mayor unknown to this large mass, who does not know the individuals in it, and who is consequently without influence and without means of action on the minds of the electors. So it is not by direct intervention, by word of mouth, as in the villages, that the agents of the government can enlighten the electors on the choice to be made, but by the sole means of the press. Hence I concluded, as I still do, that it was the press which made and will make the elections of Paris and that it was therefore necessary to capture it at all costs.'[1]

Now the press could either be suppressed or won over. It was obviously wiser to use it and Persigny obtained Napoleon's permission to win over the two great opposition newspapers of the left, the *Siècle* and the *Opinion nationale*, by making the editors M.P.s with government support. The political director of the *Siècle* was Havin, son of a

[1] Persigny to Napoleon, copy, 14.9.1865, B.N.N.A.Fr. 23066 f. 338-9.

regicide member of the convention exiled by the restoration, member of the liberal opposition in the parliament of the monarchy of July. Pursuing his course leftwards he obtained control of the *Siècle*, the paper with the largest circulation in France, and became an indispensable pillar of the republicans.[1] Guéroult was a St-Simonian who had with the help of his friend Jerome Napoleon founded in 1859 the *Opinion nationale*, a paper of radical and independent but not anti-dynastic views, whose circulation had in a few years risen to great proportions. These two men fell in with Persigny's stratagem, for they had little choice : if they refused to co-operate, their papers might be suppressed. For a time all went well. Their papers drew nearer to the government and quarrelled violently with the republicans.[2] Then suddenly all was ruined. Shortly before the elections the *Opinion nationale* published an article on Mexico, whose tone was such that the council of ministers gave it a public reprimand (*avertissement*). Soon after, it published an article on finance and again received a reprimand. A few days later Guéroult came to see Persigny and explained that these articles had been given to the paper by Fould himself, minister of Finance. Persigny's policy did not have his support and the plan thus came to nothing.[3]

This policy of digging the ground from under the opposition's feet was also attempted in another form. In 1857 Persigny had criticised the government for putting up a candidate against General Cavaignac. The government, he argued, should have said that whatever Cavaignac's intentions, it did not wish to oppose an honoured personage who had served his country well ; and had it caused its candidate to withdraw, it would have deprived Cavaignac's election of all political significance. It is likely that in the

[1] About 44,000 in 1866. F(18) 294.
[2] Confirmed by P. Guiral, *Prévost-Paradol*, 306.
[3] Persigny to Napoleon, copy, 21.11.1864, B.N.N.A.Fr. 23066, f. 308-10.

same way attempts were made to prevent Thiers from being opposed by the government.[1]

The sabotage which Persigny started behind the enemy's lines was, however, only one of his aims ; and no mere substitute for direct attack. He believed that a clear-cut battle was essential not only for the destruction of the opposition but no less for the creation of the Bonapartist party.[2] The revival of the old parties represented merely the return of the old leaders to politics and not a demand for liberty in the country. The proper way to deal with them was not to conciliate them, to compromise, and to allow them to infiltrate into power, as some ministers advocated, but to take one's stand clearly and unmistakably on the plebiscite and fight all its opponents. Napoleon's supporters, who were still an incoherent body formed of diverse elements, would be forced to cut their ties with these old parties and would be made into a solid party by the attack they would experience from all sides.[3]

Inspired by this belief, Persigny reaffirmed the system of official candidates and purged it of its doubtful elements. Some twenty-five or thirty of the outgoing M.P.s were not recommended for re-election, on the grounds that the government could not support men not entirely devoted to the dynasty and to the existing institutions.[4] It is claimed that this was a measure that gave proof of the intolerance and narrowness of the régime, that a M.P. had to be as a soldier and never to vote against the government on pain of dismissal. Now it is true that most of the displaced M.P.s had shown opposition and that most of them were hostile catholics ; but it is certain that there was no general expulsion of all opponents. Though Persigny was the advocate of a thorough policy, he was greatly

[1] Persigny to Napoleon, draft, 16.7.1857, Persigny papers. Cf. H. Malo, *Thiers*, 443 ff.

[2] Persigny to Napoleon, draft, February 1864, B.N.N.A.Fr. 23066 f. 254-5.   [3] Circular of 21.6.1863, F(1a) 2122(B).

[4] Circular of 8.5.1863, *ibid*.

dependent on his prefects. When therefore a prefect asserted that if such and such an M.P. was supported by the government, he, the prefect, would not answer for the election, claiming that the population was disgusted and infuriated by the M.P.'s opposition in parliament, the minister of the Interior frequently yielded. On the other hand, where a M.P.'s position appeared to the prefect to be strong, as was the case, for example, with Kolb-Bernard, a veritable leader of the catholic opposition, the government left him unopposed.[1]

Actually, mere continual support in parliament was not regarded by many timorous M.P.s as automatically assuring them of the status of official candidates at the next general election. They knew that they were probably even more subject to the danger of being ousted by rivals who had superseded them in the favour of the prefect or the minister. Thus when Isaac Pereire stood in the eastern Pyrenees, the minister announced that since he was as devoted as the official candidate, the government would remain neutral. The official candidate withdrew in protest: he was not dropped for voting with the catholic opposition.[2] In fact, many M.P.s who had voted against the government more frequently than those now displaced, remained the government's candidates.

In one case a M.P. was even dropped, not for too much opposition, but for too little. In Finistère, in face of the opposition of the legitimists and the clergy, the prefect and bishop came to an agreement to replace him. The M.P. could not but withdraw and his place was taken by a local judge of the peace, a distant relation of Carné, the legitimist Academician.[3] However, whatever the individual reasons for each decision, the general effect of the announcement of the names of the official candidates was

[1] *E.g.* A.D. Puy-de-Dôme, M.O. 1770. F(90) 375, telegram, minister of Interior to prefect of Nord, 14.5.1863.

[2] C. 1356, Pyr.-Or.; ACL 1864, 1. 308.

[3] BB(30) 431, *procureur général*, Rennes, 19.5.1863.

to suggest the mass abandonment of at least twenty of the staunchest members of the catholic opposition. Some others, having lost the support of the government, probably retired quietly from political life; but twenty stood for re-election and the election therefore became a struggle for religious as well as political liberty, and a fight between the influence of the clergy and that of the government.

Persigny could therefore enter the fray clashing his arms in an atmosphere of thunder and lightning against the black clergy and the red socialists and the chameleon-men of the old parties. The activity and the energy of the opposition made his victory all the more resounding. The most outstanding feature of the result was his triumph over the clergy. In vain did seven bishops come out publicly against the government. In vain did the clergy in some twenty-five departments enter the fray against it, canvassing from house to house, portraying Napoleon as the enemy of the Pope and of religion, and promising damnation to his friends.[1]

No purely clerical candidate of the opposition got into parliament. Thiers was defeated in three constituencies. In one of them, despite the support of the Anzin Mining Company, of which Thiers was a director and which bought a local newspaper to help him, an actual stranger to the department was preferred to him as being more likely to secure the redress of local grievances.[2] Great names like Dufaure, Montalembert, Remusat, Decazes, Casimir-Périer, Barante, Odilon Barrot, St-Marc Girardin, were soundly beaten. All but six of the expelled clerical M.P.s were defeated, after violent battles in which both sides brought into play all the known methods of intimidation and influence. The number of votes the government

[1] J. Maurain, *La Politique ecclésiastique du second empire*, 639; F(19) 5605; BB(30) 426, note (*cabinet de l'empereur*). A.D. Maine-et-Loire, 8M52; A.D. Aveyron, 1863 election file; A.D. Loire-Inf. 1M100/2. A. Chevalier to Persigny, 26 and 30.5.1863, Persigny papers.

[2] BB(30) 429, *procureur général*, Douai, 4.6.1863.

received remained the same as in the two previous elections ; and in a third of the departments it rose above the figures of 1857. Above all, the government continued to make progress in the west, and its vote there went up over what it had been in 1852, when it had not already done so in 1857. In Maine-et-Loire, Vendée, Vienne, Haute-Vienne, Orne and Eure the foundations of the Bonapartism of the third republic were being laid.

Persigny therefore hailed the election as a great victory. He might claim that there were not many more opposition M.P.s, for the old parliament had contained recommended M.P.s who had in fact formed an opposition.[1] However, there was no denying the doubling of the votes cast for the opposition ; and worst of all for him, the fact that government mismanagement contributed considerably to the election of many of the opposition members. The election of opponents in great towns and traditionally hostile regions was possibly unavoidable ; but even here it was sometimes possible to win by carefully choosing one's ground. In Bordeaux and in Yonne the old opposition candidates were supported by the government and the radicals thus kept out. Similar careful planning could have reduced the number of opposition M.P.s by at least half. In fact unsatisfactory official candidates account for several opposition victories. Great names like Berryer and Marie were confronted by complete obscurities. Buffet was opposed by a clerical whose position had been undermined by the prefect for two years, since it had been expected that he would be deprived of official support.[2] No doubt he was more harmless than Buffet, but had a distinguished Bonapartist been put up, the opposition would have been divided between Buffet and this clerical and the two would have been defeated. Havin likewise owed his election in

[1] Circular, 21.6.1863, F(1a) 2122(B) ; B.N.N.A.Fr. 23066 f. 254-5, Persigny to Napoleon, draft, February 1864 ; Persigny to prefects, telegram, 2.6.1863, A.D. Maine-et-Loire 8M58.
[2] BB(30) 430, *procureur général*, Nancy, 26.5.1863.

no small measure to the government's undermining the position of his opponent, the official candidate, in accordance with the plan to adopt Havin. The government found a candidate to oppose Ancel only a fortnight before the election, which was far too late. The mayors of this constituency included many retired merchants of Havre, clearly disposed in Ancel's favour and several years of preparation were obviously required to overthrow him.[1] Again, in Loiret, Persigny sought to evict Grouchy from a constituency in which he had been sub-prefect for fifteen years and M.P. for six; where he consequently had one-third of the mayors and one-half of the judges of the peace on his side. The government was thus deprived of its normal electoral agents but took no measures to prevent the inevitable result.[2] In three constituencies the new official candidates were unpopular choices, either as strangers to it, or as a subject of local hates and rivalries which deprived them at the outset of many votes.[3] In two others the government was defeated largely because the official candidates had been drugged into sleep by long unchallenged possession and just did nothing to secure re-election.[4] Chambrun might well have been defeated had the prefect not published at the last moment a brusque telegram from the minister of Education saying that he would not tolerate the hostility of the clergy. On the last night almost every house was therefore visited by the priests and the balance tipped in their favour.[5]

Those who disagreed with Persigny used the large figures of the opposition votes to attack him. 'The evil', wrote Baroche to Napoleon, 'is in a great degree the result of the direction given by the minister of the Interior to the

[1] BB(30) 431, *procureur général*, Rouen, 25.5.1863 and 18.6.1863.
[2] BB(30) 430, *procureur général*, Orléans, 8.6.1863.
[3] BB(30) 429, *procureur général*, Douai, 4.6.1863 and 17.6.1863; A.D. Nord M30/10, sub-prefect, Cambrai, 9.3.1863.
[4] BB(30) 429, *procureur général*, Douai, 4.6.1863.
[5] F(90) 589, prefect of Lozère to minister of Interior, 3.6.1863. A.D. Lozère IV M 14, prefect, 28.5.1863.

electoral campaign and to the violence with which some were supported and others fought. . . . The government of the emperor is strong enough to have no need either of such agitation or of such a great deployment of circulars and newspaper articles, or, above all, of violence to obtain from universal suffrage M.P.s frankly devoted to the imperial dynasty.'[1] Even those who were not biased against Persigny's general policy recognised that the main lesson of the election was that the official candidates should be selected with more care and that greater attention to local details would have prevented many defeats.[2]

It was this violence on the one hand, and lack of attention to detail on the other, which led to Persigny's dismissal. 'Your maintenance in office', Napoleon wrote to him, 'will cause the agitation to continue, it will excite opinion and make the verification of the elections disastrous for the government. What do you want people to say in support, for example, of the candidatures of MM. Seneca and Boitelle, discredited men who were elected only as the result of the most culpable pressure of the administration! Well, I say it with regret, your temporary withdrawal can alone re-establish calm in public opinion. I recognise the great devotion you have shown me and I am far from bearing you any grudge for not having succeeded everywhere. But it must also be acknowledged, your superior and lucid mind is worthless for administration where all must be prepared long before by perpetual regular conduct. How could you succeed, for example, when the candidature of M. Delessert was improvised ten days before the election . . . ?'[3]

[1] Draft dated 1863, Baroche papers, 1014 f. 36-42.
[2] BB(30) 427, *procureur général*, Aix 8.6.1863 ; *ibid.*, *procureur général*, Amiens, 6.6.1863 ; BB(30) 429, *procureur général*, Douai, 4.6.1863 ; BB(30) 431, *procureur général*, Rouen, 18.6.1863.
[3] Napoleon to Persigny, 11.6.1863, Persigny papers.

CHAPTER IX

Why Ollivier and Morny became advocates of a liberal empire and how the authoritarian empire's majority in parliament disintegrated

THERE is a myth that the liberal empire represented the abdication of Napoleon III, giving up his prerogatives in order to keep his throne; that it was forced on him by the strength of the opposition, who thus succeeded to his power. The truth is that just as the empire was founded in 1852 on a combination of forces created by the difficulties of the republic, so likewise the liberal empire was the result of a regrouping of these forces under the new circumstances created by fifteen years of strong if erratic government. It was not the victory of the opposition, but of a new party composed of both opponents and supporters of the old régime. The transformation and the conversion of these men is one of the most interesting subjects of the second half of the reign. In 1857 when the five members of the opposition arrived in parliament they were completely isolated. They found that seats had already been chosen for them all alone on the highest benches of the left. In the lobbies and public rooms of the house they were similarly kept at a distance. Old school friends turned their backs and refused to speak to them. They were regarded with fear and dislike as dangerous intruders from the mob.[1] How was it, then, that the leader of this ostracised group became the prime minister of the liberal empire?

Émile Ollivier was the son of a red republican, who

[1] A. Darimon, *Les Cinq sous l'empire*, 71, 103-5.

was the friend of Mazzini and Ledru-Rollin, and who had been imprisoned and expelled after the *coup d'état*. He himself served the republic as prefect and was dismissed by Louis Napoleon. Such circumstances would have filled an ordinary man with perpetual hate of the empire and an ineradicable hostility to it. Many republicans whose careers were thus cut short by the empire had their growth completely stunted and they spent the remainder of their period of exile from power vegetating on the memory of their short spell of glory. Émile Ollivier, however, endowed with a brilliant mind, ever given to self-criticism and self-examination in its constant search for self-improvement, turned this apparent defeat into a positive advantage. He devoted his enforced retirement to study and to a complete rethinking of his position. 'Nothing is permanent,' he wrote to a friend, 'all is temporary in what we see. The hand of God is long and we must have such confidence in His justice that we must never allow ourselves to be crushed by the weight of the present, however heavy it might be. Only profit from the rest which is given you in the battle of life to subject your mind to a firm discipline. Enough of poetry, of vague reading, of Michelet, etc., etc., take substantial, hard, precise, arid books. Undertake some difficult and disheartening work, which accustoms your mind to continual effort. We have collected in our hearts enough images, sentiments, aspirations, too much perhaps! We must, to make these things useful, fill ourselves with practical facts. As Joubert, a man of parts, whose maxims I am reading, says, "he who has imagination without erudition has wings and has no feet". . . . The future belongs to us. If we have as much firmness in our will as warmth in our hearts we could plough a glorious furrow, but for this we must profit from our years of obscurity and misery to exalt our minds and create inexhaustible resources for ourselves. We shall thus become at once more learned and better: the men of the future must be saints : let us try at least to be less bad than many others.'[1]

Feeding his mind therefore not on pamphlets and newspapers, but on the best French and European classics of all ages, he grew tremendously in stature and in breadth of understanding. Gone were the dreamy schoolboy's romanticism, the politician's addiction to verbosity and cliché, the pompous façade of empty thoughts. He emerged from his studies completely transformed, imbued with an appreciation of the past and with the wisdom of the masters of politics and philosophy, but no less outstanding for the originality of his ideas and the clarity of his thought, the precision of his expression and the felicity of his style. Above all, he was no longer the typical republican or the mere politician : he had emerged with the makings of a statesman — with a new set of principles and with a definite solution for the problems of his time. The problem was how to establish liberty in France. The method so far adopted had always been revolution, but revolution inevitably produced reaction and France thus moved perpetually between absolutism and anarchy. Nothing firm could be founded on a revolution. Reforms must be gentle and gradual if they are to succeed : they require a basis of peace and good order and they must seek to rally all the classes of the nation. Revolution was essentially violent, and made half the nation opposed to its reforms from the beginning. Ollivier's paramount aim was liberty and therefore, since he could not establish it by revolution, he saw he must accept the existing régime. He would not be 'wedded or glued to forms of government' : he had personally preferred a republic, but if the empire granted liberty and was willing to concede the principles, which was all that mattered, there was no reason why he should insist on the outward form. His opposition must be honest : he must show that he was opposing because he

[1] Ollivier to Guiter, 18.12.1849, and 15.6.1852, copies, Ollivier papers.

wanted the triumph of his ideals and not because he had been expelled from office and wanted to regain his place.

He proclaimed a new policy of constitutional opposition, and announced his readiness to rally to the empire if it became liberal, to help it in the disinterested task of reconciling liberty and order in France. He worked out a definite plan for the creation of a new party. 'In the legislature', he wrote in 1859, 'I shall confine myself . . . to resuming my work, modest, thankless, slow, but whose grandeur and usefulness posterity will recognise, because from it will date, I hope, a *liberal* republican school, reasonable, possible, immoveable in its convictions . . . whose leaders . . . will understand that a deserved defeat is not mended by sitting with folded arms and declaring oneself *indignant* at it.'[1]

His constructive policy made him break with the various groups of the republican party in turn. By entering parliament and taking the oath to the empire, he divorced himself from the old men of 1848 and from those who refused to have anything to do with a government tainted with the original sin of the *coup d'état*. By welcoming the liberal measures of 1860 as one of the greatest reforms a government had ever carried out on itself, and by declaring that if Napoleon went on to introduce liberty, he would support him, he dissociated himself from the systematic opposition and founded a new school of constitutional opposition. Finally, when he co-operated with the government in 1864 in the reform of the law of combination and in 1865 voted for the address to the throne to prove the sincerity of his willingness to accept the empire, he broke with Jules Favre and the 'irreconcilables'.[2]

He thus lost nearly all his old friends, but he had all the time been gaining new ones, and winning an ascendancy

[1] Ollivier to Guiter, 22.7.1859, copy, Ollivier papers.
[2] É. Ollivier, *Le 19 Janvier*, 187-91 ; Ollivier's diary, 14.7.1849, 7.12.1849, October 1857, August 1864.

over the rest of the house and the loyal official candidates. When he had first come to parliament they had been determined not to listen to him, and to silence him with their coldness and indifference. His very first speech, however, won their attention and their admiration, for he had made moderation and disinterestedness his studied principles and he at once showed himself to be no violent red. He was a great speaker to whom it was impossible not to listen. He dazzled the house with his ability to master a subject at the shortest notice; he charmed it with his smooth flowing oratory and by his lucid exposition carried it with him. In 1858 Montalembert heard Ollivier speak in parliament and noted in his diary, 'This young democrat will go far. . . . By his moderation he puts out even . . . Granier de Cassagnac' (a leading ultra-right M.P.). Montalembert asked to see Ollivier, and wrote after the meeting, 'I am very struck by the distinction and loftiness of mind of this orator in the making. He is to all appearances *a real liberal*, which is perhaps rarer in the ranks of the democrats than anywhere else.'[1]

Finally what enabled Ollivier to move towards the empire was the fact that, unlike Thiers, who could rival him in his influence on the house, he did not believe in pure parliamentary government. He had quarrelled violently with Thiers because he objected to the latter's maxim that 'the king reigns but does not govern'. 'Ministerial responsibility', he wrote in 1861, 'means royal inviolability. Now this is the monarchical principle and not the republican or democratic principle. Democratically every act carries a responsibility with it.' 'Just as representative government is great, so parliamentary government is despicable.' The ministers must have a place in parliament but they must not depend for their existence on the votes of the house. If parliament defeats the

[1] É. Ollivier, *Le 19 Janvier*. 175; M. Du Camp, *Souvenirs d'un demi-siècle*, 1. 226, 237-9; Montalembert's diary, 18. and 23.2.1858.

ministry, the king dismisses it if he thinks parliament is right; but if not, he dissolves and appeals to the country. In practice of course he would not find it in his interest to keep in office ministers who were unpopular. Parliament must impose not men but principles on the executive. What we want therefore, said Ollivier, is not parliamentary government which absorbs the executive power or leads to revolution, but the end of absolute power and the return to the representative system — *i.e.* the system founded on free elections and an independent press. Liberty alone was no use. 'Liberty but also democracy. Without liberty, democracy is nothing but despotism. Without democracy, liberty is nothing but privilege.' As early as 1861 therefore, Ollivier is found preaching the self-same doctrine which he put into practice in 1870.[1]

Ollivier was at the same time encouraged to hope that Napoleon would concede more liberty by the duc de Morny, who likewise played a leading role in the creation of the liberal empire. Morny has generally been misjudged, for he put very little down on paper; he has therefore remained enigmatic, like Napoleon III, and been considered a mere dilettante and speculator. Now it is true that he was not endowed with a brilliant mind nor with any gifts of oratory and that he could not impose his will by the force of any intellectual superiority. But in politics it is frequently more useful to be liked than to be admired, and Morny, as an essentially likeable man, who could make friends at once by the charm of his manner, who could influence them by his sound common sense free from pretension, and who could keep them by his conciliatory spirit and his intuitive appreciation of the point of view of others, was one of the empire's greatest assets. It was all very well satisfying the masses and silencing the leaders of the opposition, but government is a co-operative enterprise which depends for its success on keeping its

[1] Ollivier's diary, 10.4.1861 and 27.11.1861.

personnel together. Morny was just the man to do this. 'He had always thought,' he told parliament in 1856, 'and he is more than ever convinced that the most carefully thought out constitutions, the most far-seeing standing orders, must, in order to function well and for long, have the co-operation of men, their good will, their good faith and their good sense. . . .' Parliament and government would be kept in agreement not simply by institutions but also by men.[1]

With such a nature and such views, Morny was invaluable in managing the legislature. 'M. de Morny', wrote Granier de Cassagnac, 'had as a characteristic a taste for creating a clientèle of friends whom he strengthened with his influence and whose action added weight to his own authority. He was careful besides to choose men who were not only devoted but also distinguished. It was thus that he succeeded in dominating the legislature till his death. He had formed a group of twelve colleagues there who, at a given moment, moved quietly along the benches and caused his opinion to prevail among them.'[2] The M.P.s found a protector and a counsellor in him. When, for example, one of them was attacked by the administration in his constituency, Morny wrote thus to the minister of the Interior, 'If your prefects persecute my M.P.s, how can you expect me to preside over the house in a manner profitable to the emperor and his government? I beg you, for mercy's sake, in the general interest, to take no decision on any of them without at least having discussed it with me.'[3] He conducted the debates of the house with great skill and smoothed the path for many a measure by his tactful handling. He owed his success not least to his taking advance action to prevent all the difficulties he could foresee from arising. One day, for example, he said

[1] CRCL 1856, 138-9 ; PVCL 1858, 1, annexe 7.
[2] Granier de Cassagnac, *Souvenirs*, 2. 96-8.
[3] Morny to Billault, 14.7.1855, Billault papers.

to a liberal M.P., 'Is it true that your friends intend to be very violent on the Mexican question?'

'I think they want to pull it to pieces.'

'My God!' said Morny. 'No one wants the end of this expedition more than us. But if the opposition presses us too much, the government will certainly be forced to persevere. Let the opposition show intelligence and patriotism, let it help the government to get out of the hornets' nest into which it has thrust itself. Is that asking too much?'[1]

As the opposition increased and as the government faltered, it became more and more difficult to manage the house. Morny advocated liberal concessions, not from mere weakness, but from a positive belief in their desirability. 'A government not subject to control or to criticism is like a ship without ballast. The absence of contradiction blinds a government and sometimes leads it astray, and it does not reassure the country.' The system of having ministers responsible only to the emperor was bad, since it freed them from the control of their colleagues and placed the responsibility for all they did on the emperor.[2]

Morny was in fact very much like the Tory country gentlemen who were passing reform bills on the other side of the Channel. He was a conservative who knew how to swallow liberal pills when it was necessary. He believed in concession almost as in a principle. Shortly before the revolution of 1848 he had said, 'Since my entry into this house, I have been a very sincere partisan of parliamentary reform and nevertheless I have remained a faithful conservative. Nothing is more demoralising for a country than to see men changing but the government's policy remaining the same.' At the same time he published an article urging social reforms. He now wanted the empire

---

[1] A. Darimon, *Le Tiers Parti sous l'empire*, 104-6. Cf. Morny to Ollivier, 14 January(?) 1864, Ollivier papers.

[2] ACL 1863, 4. 247. Morny to Napoleon, 24.12.1863, copy of draft in M. Quatrelles L'Épine's manuscript biography of Morny.

to do what he had wanted the July monarchy to do, to act before it was too late. Charles X would not have fallen, had he not persisted in keeping Polignac, nor Louis Philippe, had he not persisted in keeping Guizot.[1]

What exactly then did Morny propose to do? A start should be made with civil liberties, which he distinguished from political liberties. He meant freedom for religion and its schools, freedom for trade unions, social reforms, the end of nepotism and of the scandals and abuses of the government. In France the government does everything, the individual must therefore be guaranteed against it. He did not want parliamentary government but he believed that the legislature should be brought into closer contact with the government to enable it to play a more fruitful role. The ministers should appear in person in parliament. 'The house will [thus] have statesmen before it and not barristers. . . . The fear of being criticised and opposed directly will make them more circumspect and more careful. You inspect things less closely when you have not got to render an account of your own conduct to an assembly and when the burden of the expense will fall on another's shoulders.' The address voted since 1860 'adds nothing to the liberty of the discussion. . . . The role of the legislature will be far more fruitful and important if it were accorded a right' to initiate laws and a greater right to amend them.[2]

Morny did not merely propose these reforms and wait till Napoleon should care to sign them. He saw the need to collect the men to put his ideas into practice. He had created his own little following, formed of members of the majority and led by Latour du Moulin (who under Morny's inspiration had written a pamphlet in favour of these ideas).[3]

---

[1] M.U. 1848, 371-2; Morny to Napoleon, 24.12.1863, *ibid.*
[2] Morny to Napoleon, copy of draft, 24.12.1863, and also note in Morny's hand from L'Épine archives, both in M. Quatrelles L'Épine's biography of Morny.
[3] A. Darimon, *L'Opposition libérale sous l'empire*, 72.

However, as he said, 'The forces of democracy will always grow, we must satisfy them in order not to be carried away by them'; and what he wanted to do therefore was to effect a 'fusion of [the government] and democracy for the organisation of liberty'.[1] The obvious man for such a fusion was Ollivier, who not only shared these ideas but would provide the essential parliamentary leader.

As early as 1863, therefore, and on several occasions later, Morny urged Ollivier to join him in a ministry to carry out his programme. He suggested founding a news-paper, for which he would find the money and which Ollivier would edit, to publicise their ideals. He offered decorations to Ollivier and Darimon and eventually got the latter to accept as open proof that he was sincerely willing to co-operate with the government. He tried to get a member of the dynastic opposition elected to the office of secretary of the legislature and succeeded at the third attempt. He prepared them for the leadership of the house by getting Ollivier appointed reporter of the law of combination, which was to be the first of his projected civil liberties. Before his death he was planning more such moves to prepare the way for Ollivier's passage from opposition to the government.[2]

Ollivier was on various occasions asked for the condi-tions on which he would enter a ministry, but a liberal ministry was impossible until a liberal party had been created in its favour, and that is why it took five years from Morny's death before the liberal empire could be founded. It was no use for Ollivier to join a ministry by himself: he must enter it as the leader of a majority.

The years 1863 to 1869 witnessed the gradual formation of such a majority. It was not formed simply from men of the opposition and this is the most important point about it.

---

[1] Ollivier's diary, 27.6.1863.
[2] Ollivier's diary, 27.6.1863, 17.2.1864, August 1864, 2.1.1865. É. Ollivier, *Le 19 Janvier*, 219; A. Darimon, *Le Tiers Parti sous l'empire*, 38-9, 187.

Had the republican opposition been returned victorious at an election, it would have been met either with an abdication or with a *coup d'état*. Napoleon could only share his power with a dynastic majority. What happened now was that some of the opposition accepted the dynasty and some of the majority moved towards them and became supporters of a liberal empire. This regrouping of the house was due first to the rise of new issues which divided it in new ways — above all, ecclesiastical policy, free trade and the pace of liberal reform. It was due secondly to the absence of clear leadership from the government. The separation of the executive from the legislative had placed the majority in a curious position. They were not called upon to defend the government, and were usually content merely to register favourable votes. The few opposition members spoke almost as much as the whole majority, at least on important questions, and ministers and counsellors of state answered them.[1] There was no real partnership between the ministers and the members of the majority, who were therefore more willing to follow leaders in the house itself who could put forward definite programmes in which they could participate.

Thiers began forming a group almost as soon as he got into parliament. He kept it separate both from the irreconcilable left and from Ollivier's following; but it was composed mainly of clericals and of men elected against the government, who would accept the dynasty grudgingly only if it granted parliamentary government.[2] Hence, for all the prestige he enjoyed, he could not form the nucleus of a majority with them. Ollivier, meanwhile, was working in another direction. He could not go back to the left, with whom he had completely broken, and it was useless remaining isolated. 'The best plan for us is to mix as

[1] Cf. ACL 1862, 2. 73-4.
[2] A. Darimon, *Le Tiers Parti sous l'empire*, 60, 66, 85, 87; Ollivier's diary, 4.6.1863.

much as possible with the liberal elements in the house',
that is, those who wanted the crowning of the edifice. At
the end of 1865 therefore, he held a dinner at the house of
Janzé, an official candidate who had broken with the government because of his excessive liberalism, for the purpose of
organising a liberal empire party. Those present included
another official candidate, and it was hoped to recruit still
more like Welles de La Valette and Jules Brame.[1] Morny's
friend Latour du Moulin, convinced likewise that it was
unwise to form a third party 'from outside the majority',
was moving in the same direction and various other
official candidates began to vote with the opposition.[2]

While the liberals were causing the disintegration of
the majority from one side, Jerome David began pulling it
to pieces from the other side by organising a right-wing
party. The club of the *rue de l'Arcade*, which had started
as a gathering for members of all parties, had elected him
president; he began to use it to influence their politics; he
conveyed messages to them from Rouher; and gradually
secured the departure of all but the ultra members.[3] Here
is an example of how he acted. 'Yesterday', wrote Geiger,
a loyal Bonapartist, 'Jerome David took me aside to confide
to me that he wanted to write a letter to the emperor by
which he hoped to have the bills on the press and public
meetings withdrawn, if the letter was signed by 80 or 100
members of the majority. He appealed to my devotion,
which he seeks in certain simpletons only to forget it later;
he let me understand that the empress was in agreement
with him; in a word, it was a little intrigue to become
minister being hatched under a petticoat.'[4]

These groups gradually became more and more united
and defined, though of course they always remained without any permanent organisation or discipline. The election

---

[1] A. Darimon, *Le Tiers Parti sous l'empire*, 330-1.
[2] A. Darimon, *Les Irréconciliables sous l'empire*, 30.
[3] *Ibid.*, 49-54, 142, 180, 188.
[4] Geiger to Persigny, 26.11.1867, Persigny papers.

of the secretaries of the house became a party struggle, with each group trying to secure the nomination of one of its members. Above all, the habit of voting with the government grew weaker. When laws were rejected by the house, it was a sign of independence rather than of party organisation. What really broke the majority up was the amendments and interpellations. Groups of M.P.s went about recruiting support for their ideas; the signatories of amendments acquired cohesion and began to vote together again and again. Once a member of the majority had been got to vote independently a few times, his independence became a habit. He ceased to be a member of 'the compact majority', as Latour du Moulin called it, and became 'an occasionally dissident member of the majority'.[1]

The session of 1864 saw the first step in the creation of the liberal empire group: Ollivier as reporter of the law of combination openly co-operated with the government and broke with the left. In the following year sixty-one votes were cast for an amendment in favour of subjecting the press to the control of the courts instead of to that of the administration.[2] Another amendment sought to enumerate what the opposition wanted from the law of decentralisation which the government had promised, instead of merely thanking it vaguely in the address to the throne. It obtained only twenty-five votes, but forty-two M.P.s abstained, showing that, though they agreed with the content of the amendment, they were unwilling to appear to dictate to the government.[3]

In 1866 the decisive step was taken. Ollivier drafted, with the co-operation of Chambrun and Buffet, an amendment to the address, asking the government to proceed to the crowning of the edifice. The organisers collected signatures only from men whose dynastic loyalty was not suspect, and Ollivier himself preferred not to sign it in order not

[1] ACL 1868, 7. 25.   [2] ACL 1865, 2. 191.
[3] ACL 1865, 2. 293 and 3. 30.

to frighten away any members of the majority who, though favourable, would be unwilling to co-operate in any opposition. When the amendment was discussed, a member of the right wing said that it was 'a defiance against the sovereign' — to which Buffet retorted, 'No, no, sir' — a protestation of dynastic loyalty which made a great impression on the house. Forty-two signatures were collected, which included a few more recruits to the 'dissident majority', and more would have signed had they not objected to dictating a programme to the emperor.[1]

These scruples diminished with the increased uncertainty of government policy. The government did indeed embark on a programme of liberal legislation, but this was not supported by some of the ministers : it was opposed by the right wing ; and the left found it inadequate. There were delays, postponements and talk of withdrawing the bills. The army law was very unpopular with the majority, and all the more so because it came just before an election. The independent votes in these years rose to sixty and seventy or more. Finally, in 1869, 101 votes were cast in favour of allowing the discussion of an interpellation on the government's liberal policy. These included above thirty more members for the dissident majority who were to side with the liberal empire in 1870. Thus even before the election of 1869, the nucleus and indeed over half of Ollivier's party had been formed.[2]

Just as Napoleon had taken the initiative in making liberal concessions, so too was he to a considerable extent responsible for the secessions from the majority. It was well known that he was favourable to granting more liberty and it was wise to move in the direction in which the wind was blowing. Moreover, he seemed to countenance those who took part in this liberal agitation. The night before the amendment of the 42 was debated, for example, some

---

[1] ACL 1866, 3. 240-2, Segris ; É. Ollivier, *Le 19 Janvier*, chapter 11.
[2] ACL 1869, 1. 77.

of its signatories dined at the Tuileries, and Napoleon showed no signs of irritation.[1] There was, however, no question of these members of the majority merely continuing to play the game of 'follow my leader' though to a different tune. They felt that the uncertainty about future policy, which obstructed industrial and commercial planning, and thus affected many a M.P. very closely, should go on no longer.[2] Napoleon and the creators of the empire were getting old. They must make provision for the future. The empire based on personal government would fall to pieces if Napoleon died without leaving an adequate heir. The empire must be made permanent and permanence could rest only on institutions and not on men. The youth of the country had not known the terrors of the republic of 1848 and therefore found no justification in the old despotic régime. If matters were left as they were, these young men would become republicans and the country would be plunged once more into the vicious circle of revolution and reaction. A liberal empire alone could win over these men and give new youth and life to the dynasty.[3]

[1] Articles in *La Liberté*, 2.- 7.5.1869 on the session of 1863–9.
[2] Montagnac's letter in *La Liberté*, 1.8.1869.
[3] ACL 1870, 2. 380, Dalloz ; ACL 1869, 2. 181, Louvet.

CHAPTER X

*How the election of 1869 showed the collapse
of the old system*

BY 1869 the old system of managing elections was at its
last gasp and now, what was more, the will to make it work
was slight and fitful. The general election held in this
year was far from being the last heroic fight of the dying
authoritarian régime. On the contrary, it was an election
full of confusion and of tergiversation: it was extraordinary for the way the government, though nearly
everywhere master of the ground, made terms, yielded,
withdrew, and voluntarily weakened its own defences.
For it is not less frequent for governments to commit
suicide than to be overthrown.

The circulars from the ministries sounded the first
retreat. In parliament Forcade la Roquette had insisted
that the government was entitled to use the civil service as
electoral agents, but he conceded that it had no power to
compel it to perform these extra functions. Now, in a
circular to the prefects he left it to them to decide whether
circumstances in their department made it desirable to ask
the mayors to distribute voting papers. In any case the
prefects were to avoid suspending mayors who refused to
co-operate.[1] The government thus began by abandoning
the use of one of its most important electoral instruments,
and by dealing a great blow at the power and influence of
the prefects. A considerable number of mayors now voted
openly for the opposition and with impunity refused to

---

[1] F(1a*) 2118 and A.D. Corrèze, 1869 election file, circulars of 2. and
3.5.1869.

support the government which had appointed them.[1] The minister of Education forbade his inspectors to send circulars to the village schoolmasters to stimulate their zeal, again on the grounds that the opposition would misrepresent them as proofs of oppression by the government.[2] A sub-prefect was forbidden to wear his uniform while accompanying the official candidate of his constituency on his electoral tour.[3] The support which the official candidates received was thus greatly reduced and the general policy in fact was to make them depend 'on their own opinions and personal merits'.[4] No longer was Persigny's phrase '*diriger l'opinion*' to be used, but only '*éclairer l'opinion*'.[5] Candidates thus finding themselves left to their own resources were forced to set up their own organisations, committees and newspapers.

The system of official candidates was continued but in diluted form and without real confidence in it. In the old days the minister's files were full of applications for this title: now it was impossible to find enough men to fill the vacancies. To such an extent had the opposition's propaganda penetrated that men scorned or feared to be called official candidates; and when some young man wished to enter parliament, he no longer applied to the government for this title, formerly so coveted, and formerly an almost certain guarantee of success. Persigny's trumpet title of 'candidate of the government of the emperor' was abandoned: the outgoing M.P.s had to be content to be merely 'candidates of the government'. Some judged even this to be excessively strong. Several refused it as spoiling

[1] BB(18) 1786, *procureur général*, Amiens, 8.6.1869; A.D. Isère 8M16, sub-prefect, Vienne, 31.12.1868. F(90) 591, prefect, H.-Vienne, 13.5.1869, telegram; A.N. ABXIX 178, prefect, Doubs, 22.5.1868, telegram; C.1360 Ardèche file, *passim*; BB(18) 1786, *procureur général*, Aix, 13.5.1869; A.D. Loire-Inf. 1M 100/3, report of sub-prefect, St-Nazaire.
[2] A.D. Haute-Garonne 2M36, minister of Education to prefects, 12.5.1869.
[3] F(90) 591, prefect of Creuse to minister of Interior, 2.5.1869; F(90) 408, minister's reply.   [4] F(1a*) 2118 circular of 3.5.1869.
[5] F(90) 408 minister of Interior to prefect of Côtes-du-Nord, 17.5.1869.

their chances and others made public excuses for bearing it. They were, they said, perfectly independent, even though they were the government's candidates and they made it clear that this status implied no servitude on their part. They would no longer promise 'devotion' but only 'loyal co-operation'.[1] One prefect thought it best that his candidate should avoid all such titles. Another received a letter from his sub-prefect suggesting that the title 'candidate of the government' would sound better than 'official candidate'. The prefect telegraphed, 'Say Conservative Candidate'; and then, on second thoughts, sent another telegram: 'Liberal Conservative Candidate' would be better still.[2] The wider the appeal, the better no doubt would their chances be.

A great number of government candidates did, in fact, follow this policy. Just as in the old days it had been essential for them to mention the name of the emperor, so now it was almost the rule that they should mention the name of liberty. There were, of course, many traditional professions of faith which spoke only of devotion and glory. There was one, particularly distinguished by its simplicity, issued by an old faithful, M.P. since 1852, who was, in fact, now defeated. It consisted of a portrait of the emperor, with a short statement that the candidate was devoted to him. 'If you re-elect me', it said, 'I shall, as before, support the empire and we will repeat together, "long live the emperor!!!"'[3] However, an ancient love of liberty was now claimed by candidates no less frequently than 'an ancestral devotion to the Napoleonic cause'. 'I have not for one instant', declared the duc d'Albufera, typical of many others, 'ceased to consider liberty as the

[1] A.D. Corrèze 63M, Lafond de St-Mur's circular; A.D. Maine-et-Loire 8M61, Las Cases's circular; BB(18) 1786, *procureur général*, Angers, 25.5.1869; BB(18) 1788, *procureur général*, Dijon, 31.5.1869; A.D. Isère 8M16, sub-prefect, Latour-du-Pin, 31.5.1869.

[2] F(90) 591, prefect, Pyr.-Or., 8.5.1869; A.D. Nord 30M27, sub-prefect, Douai, 29.4.1869, and prefect to sub-prefect, Douai, 30.4.1869.

[3] Travot, in C. 1366, Gironde.

indispensable right of all civilised countries . . . I want the empire and liberty.'[1] It would certainly be a different parliament which would emerge from such an election, even if all the old members were returned.

But not a few of them were not really willing to fight to the end, and in places the government would not fight at all. None of the nine seats of Paris was contested by the government and the dynastic candidates whom it favoured were careful to avoid all public connection with it. Lyons and St-Étienne likewise went undefended. Ferdinand de Lesseps, supported by the government at Marseilles, was careful to conceal the fact. In Var, a meeting of the notables from nearly all the communes of the first constituency unanimously adopted the candidature of Émile Ollivier; and before this mass defection, the official candidate withdrew.[2] Three members of the third party were unopposed in Nord, either because the government felt itself too weak, or because it preferred them to reds, who might get in if the conservatives were divided.[3] Hence the extraordinary fact that, in all, twenty-seven members of the opposition, and most of them leaders at that, were elected unopposed by the government.[4]

A year before the election, at least one M.P. was threatened with being dropped, because the government did not wish to back a loser. The minister of the Interior of the time, Pinard, urged the prefect of Aveyron to be reserved in his attitude towards Auguste Chevalier, the economist's brother. 'This expectant attitude was aimed

[1] BB(18) 1793, Eure; cf. A.D. Corrèze 63M, Mathieu; BB(18) 1788, Cornudet in Creuse; C.1364, Boudet in Dordogne; BB(18) 1790, Dumas and André in Gard, etc.
[2] F(90) 591, prefect of Var, 5. and 8.5.1869; F(90) 408, minister to prefect of Var, 13.5.1869.
[3] A.D. Nord, 30M25, prefect's letters, 25.2.1869 and 14.5.1869.
[4] Gambetta, Thiers, Bancel, Picard, Garnier-Pagès, Ferry, Favre, Simon, Pelletan, Raspail, Dorian, Buffet, Brame, Kolb Bernard, Chevandier de Valdrôme, Ollivier, Plichon, Tillancourt, Malezieux, Martel, Estourmel, Laroche-Joubert, Planat, Magnin, Marion, Tachard, Grévy.

at giving you time to study with complete moral freedom the real inclinations of public opinion. It was aimed in addition at allowing the government to clear itself of responsibility by withdrawing from the fight if the re-election of the sitting member was found to be too seriously endangered . . . and to avoid exposing the government to a serious political setback which might occur if it rashly gave him its patronage.'[1]

This fear of being beaten caused the government to adopt as its own a handful of candidates who were more liberal than dynastic. In Bordeaux the trick of 1863 was repeated and a liberal was successfully chosen to prevent a radical being elected.[2] In five other constituencies the official candidates were not elected at the first ballot, and another ballot was necessary : but such was their discouragement that they withdrew and the opposition was victorious. A sixth man was prevented from following them only with difficulty.[3] In three cases where a second ballot was necessary, the government declared its support for one of the independent candidates, in order to avoid a radical.[4] Thus, almost exactly half of the opposition or independent candidates entered parliament with, as it were, the co-operation of the government.

In the majority of cases the government did not of course yield but it had nevertheless given the opposition the weapons with which to fight. Liberty of the press and of meeting benefited the opposition alone, and produced a campaign conducted with a violence unprecedented since the second republic. In Paris 20,000 men on an average attended electoral meetings every night, in an atmosphere of great excitement which culminated in a riot and in barricades. Crowds marched through the streets, looting

[1] A.D. Aveyron, 1869 election file, minister to prefect 27.5.1868 and 20.6.1868.
[2] Houssard, Johnston, Carré-Kérisouet, Genton, Rouxin.
[3] Gros, Pouyer-Quertier, Clary, Aymé, Parieu ; and Pagézy.
[4] Baboin, Grouchy, Delahyn.

and throwing stones, crying, 'To the Tuileries'. They sang the Marseillaise, and at the line,

'*Aux armes, citoyens*',

brandished the sticks they carried. Similar violence seized the large towns.[1] The radical press reached the limits of vituperation and abuse. Revolution seemed at hand. There are historians who assert that all this produced a reaction in the government's favour, which resulted in all conservatives rallying to the government's support to defeat the reds : the election, they assert, was therefore one of conservatism against radicalism. This is not the case. The challenge of the reds was far less marked in the provinces and certainly the parties did not call a truce in the government's favour. The clergy did not support the government with any concerted plan. They based their choice, as always, largely on the personal merits of each candidate. Though the bishops frequently pledged their support to the government, the clergy more frequently aided the clericals and legitimists. Where there were second ballots, they usually transferred their votes to the government. But the spirit of conservatism could hardly have been dominant among them if the *Univers* did not hesitate to say, 'Since nothing can be expected from him, it does not matter defeating M. Pons Peyruc [the official candidate in Var], even if it benefits a radical'.[2]

Never before had there been so many candidates. There were 333 for the nine seats of Paris alone.[3] A bare 10 per cent of the seats were not contested. If the opposition candidates who got a decent number of votes and can be taken seriously are counted, the totals are as follows in round numbers and omitting those who cannot be classified.

[1] A.N.45 A.P.5, reports of prefect of police. F(90) 591, prefect of Bouches-du-Rhône, 20.5.1869.
[2] J. Maurain, *La Politique ecclésiastique du second empire*, 908 and 910. F(19) 5606, note, ministry of Religions.   [3] C.1374.

Republicans	140	Catholics	20
Legitimists	45	Liberals	40
Orleanists	30	Dynastic	25

The results of the election gave the government a nominal victory, though it is the great increase in the strength of the opposition which was more striking. Since the system of official candidates was not rigorously applied; since very independent candidates were given official patronage; and since two dozen constituencies had no official candidate, it is difficult to compare this election with previous ones. If the votes are divided between those whom the government definitely opposed, and the rest, the figures are:

Not opposed	5,105,461
Opposed	2,903,496

The government's vote here is almost the same as that in the three previous elections and it could therefore claim to have held its ground. In fact its votes must be reduced in this way:

Official candidates	4,356,510
Neutral	404,683
Benevolent Neutral	184,076
Hostile Neutral	160,192

This still leaves some independents being counted as official candidates. Nevertheless it shows that the government obtained a majority of 1·4 million over the opposition. Once again the distribution of the votes is very unequal. In thirty-three departments (and in 113 constituencies) more than half the total electorate voted for the government. The strength of the opposition is tremendous, but its division is such that the government easily won a majority in the house itself. Again it is difficult to classify members, since the election was not contested by clearly defined parties. However, the new house contained about eighty-eight independents, that is, roughly one-third of its total.

The real importance of this election is threefold. First it was a great defeat for the old Orleanist and legitimist leaders. Remusat, Casimir-Périer, Broglie, Audiffret-Pasquier, Bocher, Cornelis de Witt (Guizot's son-in-law), Prévost-Paradol, Duchâtel, Decazes, Léon Say, Passy, Falloux, Larcy, Vogüé, Crussol, Pozzo di Borgo, Carné, were all defeated. The people did not elect these men whose very names were irreconcilable with the régime. The majority of the independents were not hostile to the dynasty, except for one group, whose rise is the second main feature of the election. They are the reds, the republicans of the left of whom there were now about thirty in parliament. The old opposition was clearly split between these men and the moderates who were willing to co-operate with the empire if it became liberal. They had fought each other as well as the government at the elections, and the co-operators had returned more numerous.

Thirdly, not only was one-third of the new house in favour of a liberal régime, but a large number of the government's own candidates had in the course of the election declared their support of it too. The official candidates were thus in their turn divided between liberals and authoritarians. The old distinctions had disappeared, the forces had regrouped and an entirely new political situation had arisen. This is a fundamental point in the history of the second empire. The opposition did not defeat the government, nor win a majority to carry out its programme. It succeeded only because a large number of the government's supporters seceded and united with them. Finally, the results of this election were irrevocable because they showed that the old system of managing the country had collapsed and there was therefore no going back. The old régime was finished and the only possible solution was to create a new majority around a new régime. This was the work and the meaning of the liberal empire.

CHAPTER XI

Who supported the liberal empire and what its theory
of representative government was

THE elections showed that the old system could not be
continued, and this is why the theoretical alternative to the
liberal empire, a *coup d'état*, was impossible. But the
elections did not give birth to a clear majority able to take
office; and it took six months of negotiation before a
ministry was at length formed. The famous 116 represented the culmination of the movement which had begun
in 1866; they were 116 men who signed an interpellation
asking that the country be associated in a more efficacious
manner in the conduct of its affairs by the formation of a
responsible ministry. It was as before a coalition of the
third party and of the majority and it included only four
members of the left. The high figure was reached by
further secessions from the majority, but there were still
other M.P.s who, though favourable, would not associate
themselves with an interpellation which sought to dictate
to the sovereign.[1] In co-operation with the left the 116
might secure a bare majority to carry the interpellation,
but no government could be based on the support of the
anti-dynastic left. The 116 are therefore wrongly assumed
to be the foundation of Ollivier's ministry. They pre-
cipitated the concessions of the liberal empire, but the
largest single group was still that of the old loyal official
candidates and Ollivier had still to create a majority to
support him.

This he did in the autumn, when he appealed for

[1] ACL 1870, 2. 354, Pinard.

recruits from the official candidates. Napoleon had till then given the legislature no clear lead : the initiative had therefore been taken by M.P.s and that is why the liberal empire has the appearance of a transformation imposed on the sovereign by parliament. However, as soon as Napoleon came out of his silence and announced the liberal constitution, the official candidates became free to answer Ollivier's call, and enabled him to form a majority. The third party was swamped and seceded to form the centre left. Ollivier thus found himself with a majority composed almost entirely of former official candidates, which now became known as the centre right.

Now Ollivier intended to form a ministry based on the centre right and on 31 December 1869 such a ministry was in fact formed. It included four ministers of the authoritarian empire and the continuity between the new and the old was thus preserved in the ministry as well as in the majority. Ollivier had no wish to include the leaders of the third party. 'He talks of M. Buffet,' wrote one of his friends, 'but he confessed to me that he in no way insisted on him and that he would be obliged to make overtures to M. Buffet out of respect for his party, but with the hope of obtaining a refusal.'[1] Since each of these leaders of the centre left insisted on coming into office only together with his friends, Ollivier was not sorry at this obstinacy and formed his ministry without them. Then, however, all was spoilt by Magne demanding that the centre left should be brought in and it was in this way that the homogeneity of the cabinet was lost.[2]

The two centre parties might be allied in opposition but in office they could not work together for long. The centre right believed in a liberal empire, the centre left in a parliamentary empire : the former were more essentially imperialists and laid much stress on social reform, whereas

---

[1] Kratz to Chasseloup, 25.10.1869, Chasseloup papers.
[2] É. Ollivier, *L'Empire libéral*, vol. 12, ch. 1-7.

the latter were absorbed by pure politics and tended to be protectionists and clericals.[1] The difference between the two groups can best be seen by examining their leaders.

The father of Louis Buffet, the minister of Finance, had been a Bonapartist. He came from a bourgeois family, which included notaries, merchants and landowners, and he was himself a business man, mayor of his commune, member of the general council. He had served in the Napoleonic armies and kept his affection for the empire ever after. However, the most that Louis Buffet inherited from his father was an absence of hostility to the Bonapartes. He was born in 1818 early enough to draw his ideas from the liberal doctrinaires but too late to serve Louis Philippe. Hence in 1848 he was a pure liberal, a strong believer in the necessity of a 'régime of order, of liberty, of right and not of despotism and arbitrary power. . . . In a free country the majority makes the law and the minority must obey this law; otherwise there would be anarchy. But it is also necessary that majority and minority, that all should be able to manifest their sentiments, their opinions, their beliefs, openly and frankly, that all should be able to work by speech, press and all the instruments of fair propaganda to spread these sentiments, opinions and beliefs, to win men's hearts to them, and conquer their consciences in their favour.'[2] As early as 1851 he had rejected Napoleon's distinction between parliamentary and representative government, as being a purely theoretical one. He thought that in practice a parliament with limited powers would inevitably seek to increase them, so that it had to be either very powerful or a mere shadow.[3] His ability, his relationship with his compatriot Boulay de La

---

[1] Montalembert's diary, 12.2.1870, report of a conversation with Daru.
[2] 1848, his profession of faith, Buffet papers.
[3] Buffet to his father, 19.12.1851, quoted by Courcel, 'Notice sur . . . Buffet', *Séances de l'Académie des Sciences Morales et Politiques, Institut de France*, January 1902, 538–9.

Meurthe (vice-president of the republic), the fact that he was a new man, resulted in his being made minister in 1851, and in his learning to know and to admire Napoleon. He was, however, a parliamentarian and nothing could make him a Bonapartist; and so the *coup d'état* and the authoritarian system sent him into the wilderness. This is how he explained his conduct. 'When the *coup d'état* took place, my duty as a member of the [National] Assembly was perfectly clear', *viz.* to protest. The *coup*, however, was 'purified by the assent of the country'; and had the government then gone on to combine liberty with authority, 'I would have forgotten the past' and agreed to serve in parliament. 'I certainly did not have any personal prejudices against Prince Louis Napoleon. The kindnesses he had done me, the confidence and attachment which he had been good enough to show me on more than one occasion had found me neither insensible nor ungrateful; I would even go so far as to say that few people have had a greater affection for him, and much of this feeling still remains in my heart for him as a private individual. He will learn it if he one day falls into misfortune or out of power. It is therefore not as a result of any personal dislike, it is therefore no more because I wish to oppose for ever the act of 2 December that I keep out and shall continue to keep out of politics. No, the motive behind my conduct is to be found above all in the policy pursued since this date : the banishment of men who could be reproached with nothing except perfectly legal opposition; the decrees of 22 January [confiscating the property of the Orléans family] which are in my view a deplorable monument of iniquity, and the acts no less regrettable, which resulted in the dismissal of counsellors of state guilty of having judged according to their consciences; and finally a constitution which deprives the country of all serious participation in the conduct of its own affairs; these are the reasons which compel me to keep out of politics. As long as they continue

I shall not change my attitude. The day they disappear, I shall be completely rallied.'[1]

He was true to his word. He rejoiced at the decrees of November 1860 and returned to parliament at the following elections. He at once assumed a leading role in the organisation of the third party. During his exile from politics, he had allied with Broglie and Montalembert in founding the clerical review, *Le Correspondant*, but he had taken care not to compromise himself by any contact with the Orléans family. It was, however, inevitably towards the Orleanists that he moved after the fall of the empire, for he was *par excellence* a parliamentarian, the last of the restoration doctrinaires, believing that only men with independent incomes should become M.P.s. He died a member of the Orleanist pretender's household, and his career is thus curious in that it shows a man of Bonapartist origins becoming an Orleanist.[2]

It was the same with Daru, the foreign minister, Buffet's greatest friend. Son of a minister of the first empire, godson of Napoleon and Josephine, son-in-law of Lebrun the consul's son, he had sat by hereditary right in the house of peers under Louis Philippe, imbibed the doctrines of that régime, added to it a liberal catholicism, cast off his Bonapartism and married his daughter to the legitimist Benoist d'Azy.[3] He would enter the ministry only on condition that Napoleon told him that he did not believe that he, Daru, was an Orleanist.[4] His presence in the ministry was symbol of the general return of the men who had disappeared after the *coup d'état*. He had played an active role in the second republic, been vice-president of the National Assembly, refused ministries and it was at his house that the M.P.s met to protest on 2 December.

[1] Letter quoted by Broglie in *Le Correspondant*, May 1899, 626-8.
[2] Courcel, on Buffet, 632 and 670 ; Rouher on him, in Poulet-Malassis, *Papiers secrets et correspondance du second empire* (1880), 80 ; *Petit Phare* of Nantes, 9.7.1898.   [3] L. Buffet, *Le Comte Daru* (Paris, 1893).
[4] É. Ollivier, *L'Empire libéral*, vol. 12, 215-16.

He returned to parliament only in 1869 as opposition candidate. He represented, therefore, the half-hostile element of the centre left.

The marquis de Talhouet-Roy, minister of Public Works, occupied an intermediate position between the two centres. He was the *grand seigneur* of the ministry, an aristocrat to the core, elegant, polite, with a good word for everybody, and a passion for pleasing ; and what was more, he was immensely rich, as the heir through his mother of comte Roy, the restoration minister of Finance. He was the owner of the magnificent château of Lude, where he ruled as a patriarch, establishing model farms, draining land, cross-breeding cows and plotting railways. His sympathies and his connections were royalist : he was a director of the Anzin mines, as was Thiers, and his sister was duchesse d'Uzès. Another sister, however, was duchesse de Padoue (wife of the Bonapartist prefect and senator) and this was his link with the empire. Like Buffet and Daru, he had protested against the *coup d'état*, but, thanks to his connection with Padoue, he had been made official candidate in 1852, on the understanding that he would not be hostile to the government, though he reserved his independence and his right to criticise it. 'My devoted co-operation will be given to all that I shall think useful and glorious for France. I know that my country has need of rest. I shall not contribute to troubling it.' As soon as this need for rest became less obvious, he was of course one of the first to demand liberal concessions.[1]

The minister of Education was Segris, who owed his office to the influence he had won over the house and the important part he had played in the formation of the new majority. He was the son of a merchant of mediocre fortune, and he had married the daughter of a merchant, too. He had become the leading barrister of Angers and

[1] 'Notice' on him in the possession of the present marquis ; É. Ollivier, *L'Empire libéral*, 12. 237.

its deputy mayor when he was chosen to represent it in
1859. He distinguished himself at once by his ability; he
served regularly on important commissions and especially
on that of the budget which gave him a good preparation
for office. He was a remarkable man of great warmth and
sincerity. He gave the impression of arguing to convince
himself as much as to convince his audience, and the consequent earnestness and transparent honesty of his conclusions gave them great weight and influence. 'Mr. Segris
is one of the few orators who know how to gain over the
house and to modify its votes.' 'Mr. Segris has no tran-
scendent talent; he is not an original orator, but his speech
has a warmth so communicative and bears the mark of a
conviction so sincere, that a few words from him suffice to
disarm his opponents and reduce them to silence.' 'He
was pathetic. He used admirable gestures . . . he walked
up and down the tribune . . . his eyes wet with the tears
which the unfeigned passion he displayed drew from him.
The whole assembly hung on his lips. . . .'[1] He early
showed a leaning towards liberalism : he had been elected,
he said, to support the empire and to co-operate in the
development of political liberties. He was a new man free
from ties to any former régime, his honesty could not be
doubted, and he advocated this development with the
greatest moderation. He was no theorist or doctrinaire :
all he wanted was more participation by the country in the
conduct of government.

Louvet, the minister of Agriculture and Commerce, was
another member of the centre right who had been an
official candidate. Like Segris, he came of a merchant
family. He had founded a bank in his native Saumur,
became its mayor in 1845, and had been its M.P. since
1848. He won his ascendancy in the house by his financial

[1] *La Nation,* 12. and 26.2.1864 ; *Le Français,* 26.8.1868 ; *La France,*
15.1.1868 ; BB(6) II 391, his file ; autobiographical notes Segris in papers ;
ACL 1864, 2. 343 ; ACL 1866, 3. 240-2 ; ACL 1868, 4. 243-6 ; ACL 1868,
5. 149 ; É. Ollivier, *L'Empire libéral,* 12. 234.

knowledge, which also made him repeatedly demand more control of the budget by the legislature. 'I am one of those who think', he said in 1869, 'that no great affair which concerns the country should be decided without the participation of the nation's representatives sitting in this house. But I am one of those who think also that the best way of obtaining this parliamentary liberty, which is needed and wanted by everybody today, is to start by using the rights which we already have and so to make this liberty arrive without shock, through practice, by the force of things, and by always placing these rights under the safeguard of a close union of the sovereign and the representatives of the country.' He did not want parliamentary government, but what may be called, in the terminology of the British colonies, representative rather than responsible government. 'Without placing the government in the house, where it ought not to be, let us everywhere widen and fortify the control and the co-operation of all the elected powers', local and central. 'Let us accustom the country to governing itself.' He did not believe that the country could achieve self government by the mere proclamation of a constitution, but saw that it must be the work of time.[1] He was no mere banker but a man of culture and outstanding good sense, solid and moderate. He was, however, not a Bonapartist of race or religion : he moved among Orleanist friends and married his daughters to blue-blooded legitimists.[2]

Ollivier brought two friends of his into the ministry. Chevandier de Valdrôme, minister of the Interior, was a son of a peer of Louis Philippe and was a manufacturer of ice who had acquired a considerable reputation as a scientist. He was elected M.P. in 1859, unopposed by the government ; he had sat in the majority but had gradually moved

[1] ACL 1869, 2. 180-1.
[2] A.D. Maine-et-Loire 8M54, letter to prefect 25.5.1863 ; letter to Ollivier, 15.7.1872, Ollivier papers ; Segris to Ollivier, 10.12.1875, Ollivier papers ; É. Ollivier, *L'Empire libéral*, 12. 236.

left. Maurice Richard, minister of Fine Arts, the rich son
of a stockbroker, enriched still further by marriage, lived
as a country gentleman in the château of Millemont which
he had bought from the prince de Polignac. He entered
parliament as opposition candidate in 1863, but his opposition was moderate and his good nature made him popular
with the majority. In the cabinet he was essentially
Ollivier's man.[1]

The man who represented the liberal empire best was
without doubt Ollivier himself. The remarkable fact is
that the men of Bonapartist blood were least at home in it,
and that its staunchest supporter was a convert from republicanism. It is a paradox explained perhaps by the
difficulty of keeping an aristocracy loyal to Bonapartism.
Once an emperor has turned them into aristocrats, they
forget their maker and assume all the ideas and the paraphernalia of their new class. Moreover, the liberal empire
was based on principle and not on sentiment, and the old
Bonapartists, therefore, for whom the empire was a religion,
might join the ranks of its supporters but hardly assume
its leadership.

Now the crucial element in the theory of the liberal
empire was the question of responsibility. The emperor
and the ministers were both declared 'responsible' but the
problem was how the ministers could be responsible to
parliament if they were also responsible to the emperor,
and how the emperor could also be responsible at the same
time. It was easy to ridicule this as the product of muddle-
headedness, and as a contradiction which could not but end
in failure. The point was that it did not intend to establish
parliamentary government and that the correct analogy
for comparison is not the English constitution of the nineteenth century, but that of the late seventeenth; when the

[1] É. Ollivier, *L'Empire libéral*, 12. 238 ; Robert et Cougny, *Dictionnaire
des parlementaires français*.

king ruled as well as reigned and when ministers had to please both king and parliament. Parliament could not force any minister upon the king, but it was difficult for the king to have a minister who did not enjoy its confidence. The government was the king's government: and parliament was merely associated with him. It was no more all powerful than was the king, but the advantage was with the king, who could always dissolve parliament and appeal to the country. This is of course a much less clearly defined system, much more delicate and difficult to work than parliamentary government, since it cannot function without much tact, compromise and mutual respect. Yet since so many people believed that France was not ripe for the institutions of nineteenth-century England, it was perhaps not as silly as it might appear to start with those of seventeenth-century England.

The dual responsibility was certainly not proclaimed by accident, and was certainly not intended as a false concession of ministerial responsibility tempered by the preservation of imperial responsibility to render it worthless. Chasseloup-Laubat, who drafted the new constitution, shows quite clearly that it represents a definite theory of government. It was a theory which repudiated the principle that a king must reign but not rule. The ministers had, under the authoritarian régime, been merely grand civil servants. Now, in order to cement the alliance with parliament, the emperor would choose his ministers from parliament, from its leaders enjoying its confidence, but he would not hand over all the reins of power to them. He would continue to rule, and he proclaimed the fact by keeping the presidency of the council of ministers for himself. The ministers were his ministers for the conduct of his policy, though he would obviously find it wise to accept as his policy whatever was adopted by the majority of parliament. Ministers must therefore combine the confidence of the emperor and of parliament. Formerly the ministers, as civil servants, were individually responsible to the emperor ; now, as the representatives of the majority of the parliament, their responsibility was collective.

Napoleon's responsibility was placed above all this. He remained the elect of the people and responsible to them. This responsibility, it is true, was rather nebulous, but it was less so than the similar responsibility which the Stuarts said they had to God. On fundamental issues the emperor could appeal by plebiscite to the people. Had he abandoned this responsibility, he would have, in fact, become emperor by the will of parliament to be changed only a little less frequently than ministries ; he would have become a mere constitutional king, depending for his throne on the absence of over-excitement among the M.P.s. It was a basic belief of Bonapartism that it was absurd to leave the door thus open to perpetual revolutions and changes of dynasty. The new constitution therefore placed the question of dynasty outside the powers of parliament, and made it a matter between the people and the sovereign. In this way, it was hoped to have liberty without revolution. In this way did the liberal empire offer a constructive solution to the main problem of politics in France.[1]

[1] Chasseloup's notes on the constitution, July–December 1869, in his papers ; Napoleon to Chasseloup, 1.8.1869, Chasseloup papers.

CHAPTER XII

*What the three parties which opposed the empire re-
presented, what Bonapartism stood for, and how it
conquered a following*

WHEN Napoleon came to power there was no Bonapartist
party of any importance, but he left one behind him which
survived for twenty years. The masses who supported it
could not be accused under the third republic, as they
might be under the second empire, of merely pandering to
the holders of office and the bestowers of its favours. Is
the explanation simply that the solution he offered to the
political problems of France became appreciated and regretted only after his overthrow and after the terrors of the
Commune ? This accounted for much, no doubt, but it
is no less likely that he actually conquered the allegiance
of a great number of people who remained loyal to him.
The support the Bonapartists received was confined to
certain parts of the country. In 1877 not a single M.P. of
their party was elected in the east of France, but they had
almost complete control of the south-west and considerable
strength in certain parts of the west and north. A comparison of the elections of the empire likewise shows that
at the beginning the opposition was strong in the west and
the south; most of the south remained hostile, but the
government vote in the west increased greatly. Finally,
the plebiscites of 1851 and 1870 indicate the same change :
the west opposed in 1851 but supported in 1870. The
second empire was thus no gap in the political history of
France : it effected important changes in public opinion,
which it is necessary to explain.

It has been seen that there were politicians in office and in parliament who were Bonapartists or who had become so. The traditional policy of labelling all those who had served the empire as enemies of the republic, all of a piece, and thus making it impossible for them to forget their past, inevitably forced still more men to be Bonapartists. Certainly, too, Napoleon made an appeal to many Frenchmen as representing a principle and a system of government. All this is a matter of national politics, but in the provinces, in the conduct of daily life, politics was not a mere question of grand principles and adherence to different philosophies of life. The parties in Paris fought for clearly different forms of government, but the name of the king mattered little in the day-to-day problems with which they were faced in the country. What Napoleon did to captivate the French by his social and foreign policy is well known. But how did he act in local politics and how far did he conquer his following by his action there?

When he came to power, the three main parties, Orleanist, republican and legitimist, were already firmly entrenched in the country, each having a distinctive character. The Orleanist party was essentially a politician's party. More correctly, it was not a party at all, but simply, as a prefect wrote, a *coterie*, the sum 'of a certain number of men of merit and value who managed the affairs of the department during the eighteen years of the government of July, and who now regret the positions and the influence they have lost. . . . People have claimed that the middle classes of the towns are Orleanist, but wrongly so. They like above all their own interests and a government which protects them, and it was for this reason that they attached themselves to the government of July'. They were perfectly ready to rally to the empire if they could thus win back their jobs or at least their influence.[1] Their leaders were the M.P.s and the senior civil servants of the July

[1] F(1c) III, Ain 6, prefect's report, 2.12.1852.

monarchy who had throughout that reign indefatigably devoted themselves to obtaining roads, grants, favours, and jobs for their constituents. 'Men of such importance necessarily have a clientèle',[1] and this consisted largely of the electors of the July monarchy. Their essential characteristic, to their opponents at any rate, was not that they were of the middle class nor that they believed in parliamentary government, but that they were a clique fallen from power, formerly the dispensers and receivers of the favours of the government. In practice of course they were an intellectual and financial *élite*, and in the changed circumstances of universal suffrage, they still retained their importance. They were an army of officers and no soldiers, and could exert very little influence on the masses; but the empire could not create officers for its régime from entirely new material, and it was consequently often impossible to dispense with their services. The more violent Bonapartists claimed that the Orleanists themselves had created the myth that they were indispensable; that they owed their authority to their government and that the new government could as easily create its own aristocracy. However, they frequently continued to occupy the jobs and it was in this way that they presented a challenge to the new régime.

Republicanism, on the other hand, was essentially a popular movement. Its partisans were men who had not attained to the privilege of the Orleanists; they met not in salons but in secret societies, in clubs, factories and cabarets. Their link with Paris was not the M.P.s but the opposition press; and their leaders were generally men risen from the people. Again, devotion to the republican form of government was not universal among them. They were frequently merely radicals, liberals or opponents of the particular clique in power in their own communes, who assumed the label of 'red' because their opponents called

[1] F(1c) II 98, Ain, prefect, 30.1.1852.

themselves 'white'. 'The reds in the countryside are not always reds by conviction', wrote a sub-prefect, 'or from a desire for pillage, nor fanatics of the streets. They are more often the party opposed to the mayor, the sub-prefect, the prefect, that is, to authority.' [1] Like all parties, they had members who were made so by persecution. In the south, for example, the partisans of Napoleon I had been persecuted by the legitimists in 1815, and had therefore supported the government of July simply because it meant the overthrow of the 'whites'. When that government fell in 1848, the legitimists returned to power and, setting themselves up as the defenders of order, turned the repression of the *coup d'état* into a repetition of the white terror of 1815. 'Many of those who had been prosecuted at the fall of the empire were prosecuted a second time at its re-establishment.' [2] Such is the odd origin of some republicans. The protestants of the south were also frequently of the left simply by reason of their traditional radicalism. [3]

The legitimists combined the advantages of the Orleanists and the republicans. Their leaders were aristocrats but they had in addition a popular following and great influence on the masses. Their power as landlords and the ascendancy which the clergy had over their flocks is well known. They had an organisation to start with, in their farms and parishes; but what is less well known is the great variety of means they used to supplement the influence which they naturally possessed. Charitable organisations, religious societies and social clubs were used for political purposes. 'People are not generally aware', wrote the prefect of Vaucluse, 'that the high legitimist party, in other words the White Mountain, is organised

---

[1] Sub-prefect, Trevoux, 16.11.1852 and sub-prefect, Gex, 1.11.1852, in F(1c) III, Ain 6.

[2] F(1c) III, Hérault 9, sub-prefect, Béziers, 1.1.1853 and 4.1.1857 and prefect, 7.9.1853; note in F(1c) II 99, Hérault.

[3] Stuart R. Schram, *Protestantism and Politics in France* (1954), 90-1; F(1c) III, Ardèche 5, prefect, 5.8.1852.

here in decuries and centuries, with passwords and signs in the same way as the secret societies. Common people, workers and paupers form the mass of this association: here the Decurion is usually a foreman of a factory, [while] the Centurion belongs to the aristocracy.'[1] It appears that at least under Louis Philippe the legitimists of France were organised in regional 'priories', consisting of several departments, with minor priories for each department, and committees for the communes. Again, all these had a working-class basis, which benefited from the provident fund to which part of the subscriptions were devoted.[2] One gets the impression that whereas the legitimists of the west were dependent more on their position as landowners and on the support of the church, those of the south had more of an Italian character and used secret societies to a greater degree.

In the face of these parties what did the prefects do when, in the first days of the empire they were sent out to their departments? Their minister might want them to create a 'government party' and to send him lists of the supporters of the emperor,[3] but it all depended on the prefect. For those who were energetic and enthusiastic, the policy to follow was clear. Politics in the departments was, above all, a struggle for influence. These prefects saw the July monarchy as the nadir of the influence of the government and the zenith of the power of the cliques. Favours were granted through the M.P.s and the prefects were tools in their hands.[4] A prefect reported in 1852 that his department was entirely dominated by the legitimists and the clergy and that there was absolutely no government party. 'In the course of many years, people in this part of the

---

[1] F(1c) II 103, Vaucluse, prefect, 6.3.1852.

[2] Jeanne Lesparre, *Les Partis politiques dans la Haute-Garonne à la fin de la monarchie de juillet* in J. Godechot, *La Révolution de 1848 à Toulouse* (1948), 31-5. Cf. F(1c) III, Hérault 9, prefect, 15.10.1858.

[3] *E.g.* A.D. Tarn-et-Garonne 30M 1 & 2; J. Dagnan, *Le Gers sous la seconde république*, vol. 2 (*Le Coup d'état . . .*), 386-9.

[4] Cf. Bouvet's note in F(1c) III, Ain 8.

country have been accustomed to a complete absence of governmental direction on the part of the prefects.'[1]

Now, however, the prefects came out clothed with all the prestige which their status as agents of an all-powerful emperor gave them, and with increased powers which the decree of 25 March 1852 delegated to them. They set about re-establishing the authority of their office, 'proving to the people that in France it is the government, and in the country it is the administration which alone govern and direct', seeking to 'restore to the government its credit, its dignity and the respect which is due to it'.[2] Reflecting the conduct of the central government, the prefects sought to make all the favours of the government come to the people through them, and so destroy the power of the former ruling class by depriving it of all patronage. Yet, since they had to deal with the whole of France and not just with a small group of electors, they could not confine themselves to distributing jobs among friends. The people could be won only by material benefits, by 'perpetually carrying out useful, practical improvements'.[3] 'To excite enthusiasm here', wrote the sub-prefect of Ancenis, 'is impossible : we must give up any idea of doing so. Passions died in Brittany with the last *chouan*, but personal interests are very much alive. We shall increase the number of our partisans, and we shall keep those we have won, by obtaining extensive satisfaction for material interests. The district is exclusively agricultural ; agriculture is in distress, usury devours the countryside; we must improve its position by establishing banks for agricultural credit, funds for mutual benefit, by popularising better agricultural methods, by opening new markets, new means of communication. . . .'[4] The masses, they believed, were profoundly indifferent to politics : the people wanted plenty of

---

[1] F(1c) III, Loire-Inf. 8, prefect, 10.9.1852.
[2] F(1c) III, Ain 6, sub-prefect, Gex, 1.7.1853.
[3] F(1c) III, Gironde 6, sub-prefect, Réole, 4.5.1853.
[4] F(1c) III, Loire-Inf. 8, 7.11.1852.

'administration' in the form of such things as public works. Politics was for them 'the question of salary, work and easy living'.[1] This devotion to the material welfare of the masses was well rewarded. The empire was remembered above all as a period of prosperity, for which it got the credit, whether it was responsible or not; and the Bonapartist party of the third republic probably drew a great deal of strength from it.

The government, wrote a prefect, ought to have two aims: 'The gradual amelioration of the lot of the poor classes, who are our surest support, and the formation in the other classes of a governmental party, a Napoleonic party. In order to keep the affection and gratitude of the former, and in order to be able to work usefully for their well-being, it suffices not to abandon them to themselves, to lead them, to take up their interests. Prompt solutions must be given to the business of individuals and of communes', mayors must be chosen from elected councillors, M.P.s from among local men familiar with local problems. The second task of creating a party was more difficult.[2] It was a slow and silent process, during which the government won men over one by one. It sought to make the civil service, purged of the hostile relics of former régimes, into the compact nucleus of a solid party.[3] It adopted the methods of its opponents, too, and tried to capture whole classes of men. It organised its own charity against that of the rich, openly seeking political influence by it.[4] To the same end it established mutual benefit societies with presidents appointed by the emperor.[5] It found in the *Sapeurs-Pompiers*, the village firemen, what the Orléans monarchy had found in the National Guard — a disciplined

---

[1] F(1c) III, Ain 6, prefect, 2.12.1852; F(1c) III, Maine-et-Loire 8, prefect, 15.10.1856.

[2] F(1c) III, Loire-Inf. 8, prefect, 21.7.1854.

[3] Cf. Persigny, *Mémoires*, 301-21.

[4] F(1c) III, Loire-Inf. 8, sub-prefect, Ancenis, 1.7.1853, 28.2.1853, and 31.12.1855.

[5] F(1c) III, Hérault 9, sub-prefect, St-Pons, 22.9.1858.

force instilled with loyalty to its cause.[1] As far as possible
it filled the local councils with new men and so gave to
loyal supporters the influence which went with seats on
these bodies.

Loyal dynasties were in this way helped to found themselves in the provinces. In Loire-Inférieure, for example,
the family of Thoinnet de La Turmelière, M.P., held a seat
on the general council from 1845 to 1919; that of Gaudin,
of the Foreign Office, from 1858 to 1883; that of Ginoux
Defermon, count of the empire, from 1852 to 1932 and
again after 1945.[2] These were, however, men of wealth,
for the nonentities who were often packed into these
councils disappeared quickly enough. The problem was,
therefore, how to win men of wealth over to the Napoleonic
cause. Many prefects devoted themselves to this problem.
They opened their salons to society of all parties, and with
conciliation as their catchword they hoped to convert the
more moderate of their opponents. Being legitimist, Orleanist or Bonapartist did very often mean simply belonging
to a 'set' and an active and sociable prefect could make his
set as smart as any other and far more useful to its members.
The second empire is remembered as a period in which the
prefects were the centres of social activity in the provinces
in the same gay and energetic manner as the court of
Eugenie was in Paris; but the purpose of it all was not
purely pleasure. Balls and dinners attracted the aristocracy,
impressed the populace and enabled a prefect to pose, if he
had a mind to, as the greatest seigneur of his department.
'The government must now prove that it is running the
country,' wrote a prefect. 'I have certainly been happy to
have been able to increase its prestige by giving numerous
dinners and frequent dances in the evening. . . .'[3]

---

[1] F(1b) I 164 (2), Janvier de La Motte's file.
[2] L. Maltête, *Histoire administrative du département de la Loire-Inférieure*
(Nantes, 1948).
[3] F(1c) II 100, Lot, prefect, 20.2.1852; cf. a manuscript pamphlet in
F(1b) I 166 (33), Liégeard's file; F(1c) III, Hérault 9, prefect, 5.3.1854.

This method of winning converts was, however, not practised by all prefects. When it was used in districts where the aristocracy was powerful, there was the danger that it merely produced the swamping of government society by legitimists. A prefect would say he was conciliating them : his critic would answer that he was abandoning all influence to them. One M.P. in the west, wrote a prefect, 'belongs to the class of the bourgeoisie and thinks that, particularly in Brittany, the imperial government must necessarily base itself on the bourgeoisie or the liberal party. He regrets that the emperor's government has given the diocesan authority an influence which it did not have under the government of 1830. He does not believe that the Bishop of Rennes possesses the influence which the government assumes he has, and which he keeps only through the government's perhaps excessive good will to him. I said . . . that Mgr of Rennes was devoted to the empire and he answered that no one at Rennes seriously believed that the bishop was disinterestedly devoted. He also declared that for a very long time favours have been given only to the legitimist party, and it is because of this that a considerable part of the bourgeoisie had gone over to this party. He is convinced, moreover, that the liberal party, if it is encouraged, will give the empire in this part of the country guarantees far less uncertain than the devotion of the diocesan authority and the limited co-operation of rallied legitimists. I share [added the prefect] most of these opinions, except that Mr. de La Guistière seems to reckon a little too much on the bourgeoisie and not enough on the people . . .'[1]

The famous Janvier de La Motte, prefect of Eure from 1856 to 1869, was a supporter of this latter method and based himself on the people, rousing the 'cottage against the château'. When he came to this department, it was Orleanist, the fief of the Passys and the Broglies ; the

[1] F(1b) I 161 (25), Guistière's file, information from prefect, 5.1.1859.

Orléans family had extensive properties in it, which it had often visited and where it had made many friends. Now Janvier was a ribald, plain-speaking man who led a fast life displeasing to the prim virtue of the Orleanists, and he enjoyed vast public meetings far more than the exclusive parties of the salons. He gave huge banquets to the firemen who formed his popular clientèle. He drank noisy toasts with them to the emperor and to the prefect, and they cheered him when he said, 'The emperor is the father of firemen, of all firemen'. He was prodigal of grants and favours. 'Never have I refused anything', he declared. He spent the fortunes of two wives and ran his prefecture into a large deficit to maintain his reputation. His energy was served by great tact and a marvellous memory for names, and he acquired such an ascendancy over his department that he claimed, 'the people obeyed him blindly'. When the empire fell he became the department's M.P. In such various ways did the prefects win recruits for the empire.[1]

The basis of all these methods, however, was that all good things should appear to come from the prefect. The prefects urged that the M.P.s were simply official candidates selected by themselves, and they were very jealous of any influence which these M.P.s might gain independently of them. The influence of M.P.s, they said, could flourish under parliamentary governments; but centralised autocracy required the supremacy of that of the prefects.[2] Certain partisans of the liberal empire deplored this system and all the more so when even the prefects themselves began to complain that they could no longer manage the people as they had formerly done, and when the government itself began limiting their power. 'The prefect is no longer the dazzling star who alone spreads his light on the department;

---

[1] His file, F(1b) I 164 (2); and Robert et Cougny, *Dictionnaire des parlementaires français*.
[2] F(1c) III, Charente-Inf. 9, prefect, 4.4.1857.

he can no longer distribute favours to his friends uncontrolled; he is obliged to produce receipts to support all the parts of the budget which contain no allocations of a political character; and he cannot refuse the general council complete justifications of expenditure. . . .'[1] The effect of the prefectoral system had been, they claimed, that the government had packed the administration with its creatures and substituted them for the 'legitimate influences' of wealth. 'Now you discover that the people to whom passive obedience to the orders of the administration had been preached, on the one hand do not want to obey the administration any longer, and on the other hand they have lost the habit of taking the advice of men whom the government had fought, and so they now often accept the most regrettable leadership.'[2] They claimed that though the government was right to base itself on the masses, 'it had neglected excessively certain intermediaries necessary to winning the masses and to remaining in constant relations with them'. For example, the chambers of commerce might have been consulted when free trade was introduced. The 'intermediaries' were hurt, too, when the government chose between candidates for official investiture. This repulsed men who were ready to rally — who were legitimist or Orleanist only by tradition, which they would have forgotten on entering political life — and men who would have been glad to serve democracy outside the ranks of the republican party.[3]

In practice, however, the second empire did not differ so radically from preceding régimes. The destruction of 'legitimate influences' did not mean that it was levelling the people down and so making way for the rule of committees instead of notables, which became prevalent under the republic. For it was really seeking to replace old influences

[1] Pamphlet, *Un Préfet devant le Conseil Général*, by Boucher d'Argis, 1868, in F(1c) III, Loire-Inf. 8.

[2] Chasseloup's note on 'La Situation. MM. Rouher et Lavalette', 1869, Chasseloup papers.   [3] ACL 1870, 2. 355-8, Pinard.

by new ones. The men of the empire who came in as 'new men' immediately set about entrenching themselves and establishing dynasties just as their predecessors had done. 'We are witnessing', said an M.P., 'the creation of a new aristocracy, territorial or financial; we are witnessing the creation of a patriciate and a clientage.'[1] For, however much men might seek to work anonymously for the government, energetic individuals inevitably conquered personal influence. It was perhaps just as well for the subsequent strength of Bonapartism that the M.P.s did not all shelter behind the prefects. The able and active ones among them became M.P.s in their own right and in no need of government support. Eschasseriaux 'was the real king of the Charentes. . . . I have never seen anybody know his electors and work for them like him. He kept an up-to-date electoral register of his department, I was told, on which he entered all the information he received about the life and the needs of each one.'[2] After the fall of the empire he kept his seat for ten years and was succeeded by his son. In Gers, likewise, Granier de Cassagnac dominated the prefects and the civil servants, and by the force of his personality and vast energy conquered an ascendancy also bequeathed to his sons.[3] They founded papers of their own with which to influence the masses and the services they rendered won them a host of loyal devotees. They allowed the electors to suppose, complained a prefect in 1865, that 'their position as controllers of the acts of the government gives them a right of surveillance and almost of tutelage over the administration. They are already seeking to anticipate the time when their re-election will be achieved with their personal strength; and to this end they will do all they can to seize on the various questions

---

[1] ACL 1864, 2. 333-6. Cf. Rigaud's file BB(6) II 366.

[2] Jules Richard, *Le Bonapartisme sous la république* (2nd edition, 1883), 154.

[3] Cf. J. Dagnan, *Le Gers sous le second empire, 1869*, in *La Révolution de 1848*, vols. 29 and 30, 6 articles.

which will embarrass the departmental administration and will try to prove that everything has to be done through their influence. Not a job will be given without their insinuating the idea that they had almost been responsible for the appointment themselves.' Here someone in the ministry noted in the margin, 'This is a tendency which increases more and more on all the benches of the house'.[1]

It is clear, therefore, that the Bonapartism of the third republic was not based simply on deluded memories of the good old days of the empire, but on definite and tangible achievements. Now from what parties were its supporters recruited? Only a small proportion could have been Bonapartists of the first empire. Under Napoleon I the east was Bonapartist and Normandy royalist, whereas under the third republic the east was republican and Normandy Bonapartist. Tarn-et-Garonne, it is said, was one of the most anti-Bonapartist areas of France under the Hundred Days, but it was Bonapartist under the third republic.[2] There may be some continuity in the Bonapartism of Charente-Inférieure, but Dordogne, its neighbour, which, in 1877, elected six Bonapartists and only one royalist, had no Bonapartist past. There is the additional circumstance that, apart from the Charentes and Corsica, the departments which acclaimed Napoleon most unanimously in 1851, no longer supported him with anything like the same enthusiasm in or after 1870.

It may be that the transformation effected by the second empire proceeded on some such lines as these. The Bonapartists probably gained at the expense of the legitimists, whose influence was diminished by the disintegration of their great properties and by their abstention from office.[3] The peasant, too, was emancipating himself from his lord. 'The peasant who sixty years ago owned nothing,

---

[1] F(1c) III, Charente-Inf. 13, prefect, 1.5.1865.
[2] Le Gallo, *Les Cent Jours*, 368 ; J. Vidalenc, *Le Département de l'Eure sous la monarchie constitutionnelle*.
[3] Cf. F(1c) III, Maine-et-Loire 8, sub-prefect, Segré, 6.7.1858.

is today everywhere a landowner.   Henceforth his interest prevails over old traditions.   When the wastelands were divided, as was generally done in Loire-Inférieure, he nearly always found the local aristocracy as his antagonist, either because it renewed old claims or because it exhumed old title deeds, or because it used the fact of its possessing extensive properties to claim a proportionately larger share.   The peasants have preserved the memory and the grudge.   They are happy to reach municipal office, which gives them some authority over the descendants of their own lords.   The influence of the nobility in the countryside received a first blow in this way.   Every electoral defeat since has reduced it further.   Forced to live on his own capital, obtaining no part of the profits of commerce or industry, or from the salaries of administrative offices, it has gradually fallen into debt — the registry of mortgages tell to what a degree. Finally, by refusing the oath and abdicating all participation in the deliberations of our councils and our assemblies, it has given itself the final blow.   All these circumstances do not escape the perpetual attention of the peasant.   For him, words are not enough, he needs deeds.   Placed between the promises which have for over twenty years announced an ever postponed restoration, and the acts of the empire, at once energetic and benevolent — he is almost converted to new ideas which daily effect new progress and new benefits for him under his own eyes.' [1]

When the legitimists were not supported by a powerful clergy, the Bonapartists were frequently able to gain ground, and it is precisely in the non-clerical areas of peasant proprietors that they struck root under the third republic.[2]   They probably also obtained their share of the liberals of the constitutional monarchy in areas where the legitimists were even more reactionary than the Bonapartists, and where, therefore, the liberals would support

[1] F(1c) III, Loire-Inf. 8, sub-prefect, Ancenis, 28.2.1853.
[2] Cf. A. Siegfried, *La France de l'Ouest sous la troisième république.*

them as standard bearers of the tricolour against their ancient white enemies. More liberals, however, probably went over to republicanism because of the way the empire was founded. A map showing the arrests which followed the *coup d'état* coincides largely with what was later a republican area. Bonapartism was not liberal but democratic: it appealed more to those who wanted to bring the aristocrats down than to the professional men of the liberal party who wanted to climb to social distinction.

However, these generalisations about the Bonapartism of the third republic may be similar to those which men make about that of the second empire before they undertake its study. The Bonapartism of the third republic must be left for another time. It is enough if this book has shown the interest of its parent, and given some insight into the meaning of politics before the great watershed of 1870.

MAPS ILLUSTRATING THE DEVELOPMENT
OF BONAPARTISM

THE PRESIDENTIAL ELECTION OF 1848

Departments in which Cavaignac got a majority of the votes cast.

Departments in which Cavaignac got over 25% of the votes cast

Based on results published in 'Proclamation de Louis Napoléon Bonaparte' 1848,
B.N. Lb(55)17

The opposition to Napoleon in 1848 is in the west and south; the outlying departments on the periphery of the country seem to be standing out against Napoleonic centralisation

THE PLEBISCITE OF 1851

PAS DE CALAIS
NORD
SOMME
SEINE INFRE
AISNE ARDENNES
OISE
CALVADOS EURE
ORNE
SEINE ET OISE
SEINE ET MARNE
MARNE
MEUSE
MOSELLE
BAS RHIN
MEURTHE ET MOSELLE
CÔTES DU NORD
FINISTÈRE
ILLE ET VILAINE
MORBIHAN
MAYENNE
EURE ET LOIR
SARTHE
AUBE
HTE MARNE
VOSGES
HT RHIN
HTE SAÔNE
BELFORT
LOIRE INFRE
MAINE ET LOIRE
LOIR ET CHER
LOIRET
YONNE
CÔTE D'OR
DOUBS
DEUX SÈVRES
INDRE ET LOIRE
CHER
NIÈVRE
SAÔNE ET LOIRE
JURA
VENDÉE
VIENNE
INDRE
ALLIER
HTE SAVOIE
CHARENTE
CHARENTE INFRE
HTE VIENNE
CREUSE
PUY DE DÔME
RHÔNE
AIN
SAVOIE
CORRÈZE
LOIRE
ISÈRE
GIRONDE
DORDOGNE
CANTAL
HTE LOIRE
ARDÈCHE
DRÔME
HTES ALPES
LOT ET GARONNE
LOT
AVEYRON
LOZÈRE
BASSES ALPES
ALPES MMES
LANDES
TARN ET GARONNE
GARD
VAUCLUSE
VAR
GERS
TARN
HÉRAULT
BCHES DU RHÔNE
BASSES PYRÉNÉES
HTES PYRÉNÉES
HTE GARONNE
ARIÈGE
AUDE
PYR. ORIENTALES

CORSE

Departments in which under 50% of the electorate voted in favour of Napoleon

Departments in which 50-60% of the electorate voted in favour of Napoleon

Based on 'Bulletin des Lois' 1851, p.1231, no.474, vol.8, 10th series, 2nd semestre.

The strongholds of legitimism oppose Napoleon

171

THE ELECTION OF 1852

The shaded areas represent the departments in which the government candidates obtained the votes of less than half of the electorate.

Based on results in A.N., F (Ic) II 58 and C. 1336 - 1339

Again the opposition is strong in the same regions

172

THE ELECTION OF 1869

The shaded areas represent the departments in which the
government candidates obtained less than 42% of the votes
of the electorate. (They obtained 42% in the total figures
for the country as a whole.)

Based on A.N., C.1360-1378

The areas of opposition have now shifted from the west to the east,
though the south remains hostile. The map would be even more
striking did not the republicanism of the town of Bordeaux and the
independence of Laroche-Joubert (a Bonapartist of the 3rd republic)
at Angoulême make the whole of Gironde and Charente appear hostile

173

THE PLEBISCITE OF 1870

Departments in which less than 50% of the electorate voted in favour of the empire.

Departments in which 50-60% of the electorate voted in favour of the empire.

Based on 'Bulletin des Lois', 1870, p. 675-8, no. 1813, vol. 35, 1ˢᵗ semestre.

The great transformation is here clearly shown : the west, which was a principal area of opposition in the plebiscite of 1851, is almost won over. Vendée votes with the same unanimity as Corsica — over 80 per cent in favour

174

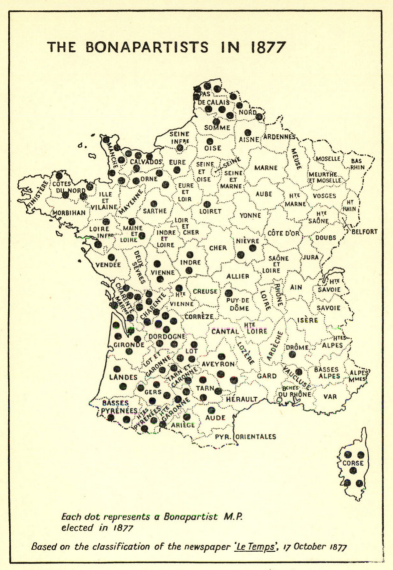

THE BONAPARTISTS IN 1877

Each dot represents a Bonapartist M.P.
elected in 1877

Based on the classification of the newspaper *Le Temps*, 17 October 1877

The Bonapartists have captured the south-west; they have penetrated into certain areas of the west and north; they are powerless in the east

BIBLIOGRAPHY

I. MANUSCRIPT SOURCES : (*a*) Public documents
                           (*b*) Private papers : (i) in public libraries
                                          (ii) in private hands

II. PRINTED SOURCES

I. MANUSCRIPT SOURCES

(*a*) PUBLIC DOCUMENTS

In the National Archives, Paris

C. 1336-1378. Results of the elections to the legislature, 1852–70, giving full details of the votes, by commune, canton and constituency. These boxes contain also birth certificates of some M.P.s ; and protests against the validation of elections, which are often of considerable interest.

C. 2708-2713. Correspondence of the president of the legislature, mainly formal.

F(1a*) 2118 and 2119. ⎱ Election circulars of the ministry of the
F(1a) 2100 and 2122 (B). ⎰   Interior.

F(1b) I 261-286. Personal files of individual members of the prefectoral corps. Full of valuable biographical information. The following files were particularly examined. Baragnon 156 (3) ; Barante 156 (3) ; Barral 156 (5) ; Belliard 156 (14) ; Berger 156 (17) ; Bigrel 156 (23) ; Blosseville 156 (27) ; Caffarelli 157 (1) ; Chadenet 157 (13) ; Chambrun 157 (14) ; Chapuys-Montlaville 157 (17) ; Corneille 157 (32) ; Corta 157 (32) ; Creuzet 157 (36) ; Dabeaux 158 (1) ; Delamarre 158 (9) ; Dugué de La Fauconnerie 158 (33) ; Fortoul 160 (11) ; Fremy 160 (14) ; Grouchy 161 (20) ; Guistière 161 (25) ; Hamel 162 (1) ; Hébert 162 (3) ; Houdetot 162 (7) ; Janvier 164 (2) ; Ladoucette 166 (3) ; Lafon de Cayx 166 (5) ; Lafond de St-Mur 166 (5) ; Legrand 166 (22) ; Lequien 166 (27) ; Leret d'Aubigny 166 (28) ; Leroy-Beaulieu 166 (29) ; Le Sergeant de Monnecove 167 (26) ; Liégeard 166 (33) ; Mariani 166 (7) ; Mercier 167 (19) ; Ollivier 169 (1) ; Ornano 169 (3) ; Partouneaux 170 (3) ; Perras 170 (10) ; Plancy 170 (17) ; Rambourgt 172 (2) ; Remacle 172 (5) ; Renouard 172 (6) ;

Roulleaux-Dugage 172 (18) ; Ste-Croix 173 (2) ; Ste-Hermine 173 (4) ; Thieullen 174 (6) ; Thoinnet 174 (7) ; Toulongeon 174 (10) ; Vilcocq 176 (12) ; West 177 (2).

F(1b) II.   Maine-et-Loire 8. Information on the personnel of the prefecture of this department.

F(1c) I 130.   Plebiscite of 1870. Results of the vote by cantons and *arrondissement*.

F(1c) II 56 and 57. 1848 election correspondence.

58. 1849–53 elections : contains some useful statistics.

59-96 (one box). 1859–80 elections, nothing much.

97. 1848–55 elections, little for the second empire.

98-103. 1852 election. A source of the greatest importance. This appears to be the only really full set of election correspondence in the nineteenth century. Letters of prefects and their subordinates, instructions of minister of the Interior and notes by his staff and others. This source has long been known but historians have never used it fully because they did not know much about the M.P.s about whom all the letters are. All this is in six boxes, arranged more or less by alphabetical order of departments. Not all the departments, however, have files in this series. Most of the missing ones can be found in the departmental series of F(1c) III.

F(1c) III.   The remaining 1852 election files are in Ariège 4 ; Calvados 6 ; Charente-Inf. 7 ; Cher 4 ; Corrèze 7 ; Corse 5 ; Dordogne 5 ; Doubs 5 ; Drôme 5 ; Gard 5 ; Gironde 4 ; Mayenne 4 ; Meurthe 6 ; Morbihan 5 ; Nord 6 ; Puy-de-Dôme 4 ; Sarthe 4 (1854 by-election only). The main interest of this series, however, is the large collection of reports to the minister of the Interior by the prefects and sub-prefects, part of them periodical and part of them miscellaneous and classed as '*correspondance et divers*'. The following boxes were studied :

F(1c) III.   Ain 3, 6, 8 and 9.
Ardèche 4, 5 and 8.
Charente-Inf. 7, 9, 13.
Gironde 6 and 9.
Hérault 4, 9, 14 and 15.
Loire-Inf. 4, 8, 11 and 12.
Maine-et-Loire 4, 8, 11 and 12.
Seine-et-Marne 6.

F(1c) V.   Departmental series on *Conseils Généraux* ; little of political importance. Loire-Inf. 5 and Maine-et-Loire 4 were examined.

F(4) 2697.   Allocations sur fonds spéciaux. What the minister of the Interior did with secret service funds.

F(14).   Personal files of M.P.s members of the *Ponts et Chaussées* :
          Boucaumont 2177 (1) ; Grouchy 2239 (2) ; Guyot 2241
          (2) ; Lacave 2252 (1) ; Lambrecht 2255 (2) ; Lejoindre
          2263 (2).

F(18) 528. List of departmental press 1883.

   307.   Subsidies to departmental press ; and reports by de-
           partment on the departmental press, 1869.

   294.   Departmental press, 1862 and 1866.

F(19) 5601. Political attitude of the clergy under the July monarchy :
            reports of prefects.

   5604.   Ditto for Second Republic.

   5605.   Ditto for Second Empire, particularly interesting for the
            election of 1863.

   5606.   Ditto for 1869 election.

F(90).   Copies of telegrams kept by the Telegraph Service.
          347, 588 and 940(B) contain those sent during the
          election of 1857 ;
          375 and 589 for 1863 election ;
          408 and 591 for 1869 election.
          These are almost entirely telegrams between the minister
          of the Interior and the prefects, but contain others of
          more subordinate officials too. In the absence of written
          correspondence they are of course very valuable.

BB(6*) 525-538 on the personnel of the magistracy before 1848, has
          little detailed information apart from dates of service,
          and hardly repays the considerable trouble involved in
          tracking men down in it.

BB(6) II, 1-434 has the personal files of magistrates after 1848 and
          these are much more valuable and more akin to the pre-
          fects' files. The following M.P.s were looked up.
          Aymé 12, Benoît-Champy 29, Denat 121, Duboys 134,
          Fabre 152, Huet 210, Laffitte 231, Lasnonier 241, Mège
          291, Pinard 339, Rigaud 366, Segris 391.

BB(18) 1567. Reports of the *procureurs généraux* on the election of
            1857.

   1786-1793. Reports of the *procureurs généraux* for the election
            of 1869.

BB(30) 426-431. Reports of the *procureurs généraux* for the election of
            1863.

   738-744. The personal files of members of the council of
            State. The bulk of the records of this department were
            of course burnt in 1870. These files are, however,
            rather disappointing. Those of the following M.P.s
            were looked up : Marey-Monge, Maupas, Charlier,
            David, Lepelletier, Poèze and Hallez.

ABXIX 175. Maupas' report on the press, 1853.

Departmental Archives of the prefectures

These were used to fill in the gaps which the central archives have. In theory there is a draft of all letters sent to Paris in the prefects' archives, as well as the letters of the ministers, the drafts of which ought to have been kept in Paris. In fact, of course, much was destroyed or lost. Nevertheless the departmental archives proved of the greatest importance. The following files were examined. They deal mainly with the elections, and contain the usual type of correspondence to be found in F(1c) II and III but also letters of minor men like J.P.s and mayors.

Ardèche.	6 M 16 and 17 (1848 and 1849).
Aveyron.	1857, 1863 and 1869 election files.
Bouches-du-Rhône.	M (2) III 26-32 ; extracts of election correspondence of my period ; of little interest.
Charente.	M 187-192.
Corrèze.	62 M for 1863 ; and an unnumbered file for 1869.
Côte-d'Or.	3 M 72-77 for 1857 to 1869.
Côtes-du-Nord.	3 M 30 for 1857, and a file for 1869.
Haute-Garonne.	2 M 33-37 (1857–69).
Isère.	8 M 12-16 (1857–69).
Jura.	Unnumbered files on elections, especially on 1868.
Loire-Inférieure.	1 M 100/1-3 (1857–69).
Lozère.	IV M 13-16 (1857–69). Archives municipales of Mende, K 115.
Maine-et-Loire.	8 M 49-62 (1857–69).
Marne.	7 M 39 (1862 by-election).
Morbihan.	Cabinet du préfet, Série M, élections législatives, 1852–63.
Nord.	30 M 8-11 (1857–63) and 25-27 (1869).
Puy-de-Dôme.	M O 1781 (1857) ; 1770 (1861–9).
Sarthe.	M 61/16 and M 61/16 *bis* for 1857.
Seine-et-Oise.	II M 11(6) and (7) (1849–63).
Tarn-et-Garonne.	30 M 1 and 2. 'Statistique politique' of the department, listing all electors under their political party.
Vendée.	2 M 38-40 (1857–70).

(b) PRIVATE PAPERS

In the Bibliothèque Nationale

Nouvelles acquisitions françaises.

24107-24126.	Papers of Jules Favre, little of interest.
20617-20620.	Four volumes of correspondence belonging to Thiers, mainly letters received, but also some by him.

23862.   Hésèque, M.P., mainly official documents, interesting for reconstructing his career.

13177.   Gambetta's letters to his parents as a student, for light on the younger generation.

24369-24370.   Ernest Picard's papers, letters sent and received.

12295.   Letters of Haussmann to Fremy, 1850–1.

23066.   Letters (drafts and copies) from Persigny to the emperor, 1857–69.

In the National Archives

45 A.P.   Rouher's papers. Box 1 contains political notes by him, including drafts of letters to the emperor; box 2 has correspondence with the emperor and with Rouher's family; box 3 letters received on elections and other subjects; box 5 police reports for 1869 election, etc.

46 A.P.   Papers of Ducos, minister of the Marine, 3 boxes, very miscellaneous, but includes some interesting letters by him and also some from Haussmann and St-Arnaud.

In the Bibliothèque Thiers

Thiers papers.   Fonds Thiers, 1ère série, No. 24, letters from Thiers, 1824–77; No. 25, letters sent to him. 2e série No. 570, 1848 election correspondence. A great deal of valuable information.

Baroche papers.   960-1245.   The following files are particularly interesting. 979-980, letters from Fould; 981-982, from Rouher; 1000, from Morny; 1001, from Napoleon; 1014, drafts of letters by Baroche; 1015, fragment of autobiography; 1020, miscellaneous political documents; 1031-1040, changes in the constitution; 1132, elections; 1228, liberal empire.

———

Private Papers in the hands of descendants

Billault papers.   The main series is arranged chronologically with a file for each year; it contains correspondence and documents of every description which happen to have survived; of very varied importance. The second series is of letters received, most of them of no importance since the really interesting ones are in the first series. The most valuable item in these papers is the correspondence exchanged between Billault and Napoleon.

Brame papers.   Interesting correspondence with the empress; biography of him; his works.

Buffet papers.   1. Letters received, alphabetically.
2. Election correspondence, 1848–57.
3. Obituary notices and press cuttings.
4. Miscellaneous.

Chasseloup-Laubat papers. The documents used in this book come from the file dealing with his ministry of 1869, which has notes on the drawing-up of the constitution. I am preparing a biography of him which will use the rest of his papers.

Forcade la Roquette papers. About 70 letters of Forcade to his daughter, 1864–74 ; genealogies of the Forcade family ; a book of interesting press cuttings.

Montalembert papers. Diary of great interest, one volume a year, and an entry for almost every day; I examined the volumes for 1848–70.

> Large collection of correspondence, particularly with Falloux, Daru and Michel the newspaper editor.

Ollivier papers. Diary of great interest, which I shall shortly be publishing in collaboration with his grand-daughter. Written irregularly but always soon after the event and with dates given, 1846–70.

> Letters received, arranged by year.

> Copies of some letters written by Ollivier.

Persigny papers. Letters received by Persigny from Frenchmen and from foreigners, arranged separately.

> Persigny to his wife.

> Drafts and copies of letters to Napoleon.

> Letters from Napoleon to Persigny.

St-Arnaud papers. About 900 letters from St-Arnaud mainly to his wife and brother. Many deal with his African campaigns but not a few are of political interest.

> A dozen letters from Napoleon.

Schneider papers. Letters sent by Schneider from England after 1870 ; bundles of miscellaneous letters received ; and an interesting correspondence with his prefect.

> Also a valuable manuscript life of Schneider by M. Eugène Boyer.

Segris papers. Letters received, 1869–70.

> Notes for an autobiography.

> Press cuttings.

> Miscellaneous papers on his work as minister.

Talhouet papers. A letter from Napoleon, one from Ollivier, and a valuable privately printed biography of Talhouet.

II. PRINTED SOURCES

The most important printed source is the debates of the legislature and of the various parliaments of the period before the second empire.

Compte-Rendu des séances du Corps Législatif gives the summary of debates, usually one volume a year.

Bibliography

Procès-Verbaux des séances du Corps Législatif gives also the text of the bills presented to the legislature and the reports of the commissions appointed to examine them — an additional source for discovering the opinions of the house. This series consists of 5 or more volumes a year. Both it and the preceding series are published annually by the legislature. After 1861 when the debates began to be published in full the best series to use is—

Annales du Sénat et du Corps Législatif, published annually by the *Moniteur* and combining the two former series.

For the period before the second empire I used—

Le Moniteur universel, later *Le Journal officiel*, to look up the speeches of M.P.s who had entered parliament earlier. I went as far back as 1827. This newspaper gives in addition a vast amount of information about politics, laws, appointments, etc., and its editorials and the way it presents the news are often very interesting. However, its news is strictly limited and it is therefore necessary to use other papers. I looked at the following for various points which interested me :

Liberté	*Gazette de France*
Le Temps	*The Times*

Laws and decrees were looked up in the *Bulletin des lois*.

Books and articles (published in Paris unless otherwise stated) :

Comte Alexandre d'Adhemar, *Du parti légitimiste en France et de sa crise actuelle*, 1843.

Anon, *Aux mânes de l'empereur, la pairie reconnaissante*, 1840, B.N. Lb (51) 3137.

    Biographie statistique par ordre alphabétique de départements de MM. les membres de la Chambre des Députés, 1842–6. 1846, B.N. Ln (6) 49.

R. Apponyi, *Journal*, vol. 4, 1926.

A. Autrand, *Statistique des élections parlementaires et des partis politiques en Vaucluse de 1848 à 1928*, Vaison-la-Romaine, 1932.

H. Avenel, *Comment la France vote*, 1894.

    Histoire de la presse française, 1900.

Barante, *Souvenirs du Baron de Barante de l'Académie Française 1782–1866 publiés par son petit-fils Claude de Barante*, 7 vols., 1890–99.

Mgr Baunard, *Kolb-Bernard*, 1899.

A. Billault, *Œuvres*, 2 vols., 1865.

M. Boulenger, *Le Duc de Morny*, 1925.

J. B. M. Braun, *Nouvelle Biographie des députés . . . 1814–1829*, 1830.

Duc de Broglie, 'Louis Buffet' in *Le Correspondant* for May and June 1899, pp. 613–42 and 821–59.

L. Buffet, *Le Comte Daru*, 1893.

G. Buisson, *La Chambre des Députés*, 1924.

A. Chaboseau, *Les Constituants de 1848* in *La Révolution de 1848*, vols. 7 and 8, 1911.

J. D. A. P. de Chambrun, Book of engravings, B.N. Ln(27) 3836.

S. Charléty, *La Restauration*, 1911, in Lavisse's *Histoire de la France contemporaine*.
  La Monarchie de juillet, 1921, in the same series.

C. Chavanon, *L'Administration dans la société française* in A. Siegfried and others, *Aspects de la société française*, 1954.

R. Christophe, *Le Duc de Morny*, 1951.

A. Claveau, *Souvenirs politiques et parlementaires d'un témoin*. Vol. 1: *1865–1870*, 1913.

P. Corticchiato, *Les Corses et le parti bonapartiste à Marseille en 1870 et pendant les premières années de la république*, Marseille, 1921.

Baron de Courcel, 'Notice sur . . . Buffet', *Séances de l'Académie des Sciences Morales et Politiques*, January 1902, pp. 509-44 and 633-75.

P. Cousteix, 'Les Financiers sous le second empire' in *1848, Revue des révolutions contemporaines*, vol. 43, July 1950, pp. 107-35.

R. Cuzacq, *Les Élections législatives à Bayonne, 1848–70*, Bayonne, 1948.

J. Dagnan, *Le Gers sous la seconde république*, Auch, 1928.
  Le Coup d'état et la repression dans le Gers, Auch, 1929, vol. 2 of the preceding work.
  Le Gers sous le second empire, 1869, in *La Révolution de 1848*, vols. 29 and 30, six articles, 1932–34.

A. Darimon, *Histoire d'un parti*: *Les Cinq sous l'empire*, 1885; *L'Opposition libérale sous l'empire*, 1886; *Le Tiers Parti sous l'empire*, 1887; *Les Irréconciliables sous l'empire*, 1888; *Le Ministère du 2 janvier*, 1889.

J. Delarbre, *Chasseloup-Laubat*, 1873.

T. Delord, *Histoire du second empire*, 1869-75, 6 vols.

M. Du Camp, *Souvenirs d'un demi-siècle*, 1949, 2 vols.

A. Duchêne, *Un Ministre trop oublié, Chasseloup-Laubat*, 1932.

J. Durieux, *Le Ministre Pierre Magne*, 2 vols, 1929.

M. Émérit, *Lettres de Napoléon III à Madame Cornu*, 2 vols., 1937.

Esmonin and others, *La Révolution de 1848 dans le département de l'Isère*, Grenoble, 1949.

O. Falateuf, *Josseau*, privately printed, lent to me by M. Josseau.

A. de Falloux, *Mémoires d'un royaliste*, 2 vols., 1888.

A. Ferrère, *Révélations sur la propagande napoléonienne faite en 1848 et 1849*. Turin, 1863.

J. Ferry, *La Lutte électorale en 1863*, 1863.

S. Fizaine, *La Vie politique dans la Côte-d'Or sous Louis XVIII*, Dijon, and Paris, 1931.

A. Fould, *Journaux et discours*, 1867.

J. Garsou, *L'Évolution napoléonienne de Victor Hugo sous la restauration*, 1900.

Bibliography

Les Créateurs de la légende napoléonienne: Barthélemy et Méry, Brussels, 1899.

G. Genique, *L'Élection de l'Assemblée Législative en 1849*, 1921.

P. Geyl, *Napoleon, for and against*, London, 1949.

L. Girard, *La Politique des travaux publics du second empire*, 1952.

R. Girardet, *La Société militaire dans la France contemporaine*, 1953.

J. Godechot, *La Révolution de 1848 à Toulouse*, Toulouse, 1948.

L. Gouault, *Comment la France est devenue républicaine*, 1954.

G. Goyau, *Un Roman d'amitié* (Letters of Persigny and Falloux), 1928.

A. Granier de Cassagnac, *Souvenirs du second empire*, 3 vols., 1881–4.

R. Grégoire, *La Fonction publique*, 1954.

C. de Grunwald, *Le Duc de Gramont*, 1950.

P. Guiral, *Prévost-Paradol*, 1954.

D. Halévy, *Le Courrier de M. Thiers*, 1921.

E. d'Hauterive, *Napoléon III et le prince Napoléon, correspondance inédite*, 1925.

F. A. Hélie, *Les Constitutions de la France*, 1880.

P. Henry, *Histoire des préfets*, 1950.

B. Jerrold, *Life of Napoleon III*, 4 vols, London, 1874–82.

S. Kent, *Electoral procedure under Louis-Philippe*, New Haven, 1937.

Lord Kerry, *Le Secret du coup d'état*, 1928; and there is also an English edition.

P. de La Gorce, *Au temps du second empire*, 1935.
   Histoire du second empire, 7 vols, 1894–1904.

L. de La Hodde, *Histoire des sociétés secrètes et du parti républicain de 1830 à 1848*, 1850.

J. Lassaigne, *Figures parlementaires*, 1950.

P. Lecanuet, *Montalembert*, 3 vols., 1925 ed.

E. Le Gallo, *Les Cent Jours*, Dijon, 1923.

E. Le Liepvre, *Charles Kolb-Bernard*, Havre, 1893.

A. Lemercier, Obituary notice of him in *Revue de Saintonge et d'Aunis* for January 1898.

Q. L'Épine, *Le Maréchal de St-Arnaud*, 2 vols., 1928–9.

E. Levasseur, Lecture on Faucher in *Mémoires de l'Académie des Sciences Morales et Politiques*, 1910, vol. 27, 151-208.

H. Librec, *La Franc-maçonnerie dans la Loire-Inférieure*, Nantes, 1949.

S. Liégeard, *Trois Ans à la Chambre*, 1873.

H. Malo, *Thiers*, 1932.

L. Maltête, *Histoire administrative du département de la Loire-Inférieure*, Nantes, 1948.

J. Maurain, *Baroche, ministre de Napoléon III*, 1936.
   La Politique ecclésiastique du second empire, 1930.

Napoléon III, *Discours, messages et proclamations de l'empereur*, 1860.
   Œuvres, 4 vols., 1856.

É. Ollivier, *L'Empire libéral*, 18 vols., 1895–1916.
   Le 19 Janvier, 1869.

V. F. de Persigny, *Mémoires du duc de Persigny*, 1896.

A. Piette, *La Famille Piette*, Vervins, 1861.

R. Pimienta, *La Propagande bonapartiste en 1849*, 1911.

P. Poirson, *Walewski*, 1943.

A. Poulet-Malassis, *Papiers secrets et correspondance du second empire*, 1880 ed.

C. H. Pouthas, 'La Réforme administrative sous la deuxième république' in *Revue historique*, 1942–3, vol. 193.

E. Réveillaud, *Histoire politique et parlementaire des départements de la Charente et de la Charente-Inférieure, 1789–1830*, St-Jean-d'Angely, 1911.

E. Reynier, *La Seconde République dans l'Ardèche*, Privas, 1948.

J. Richard, *Le Bonapartisme sous la république*, 2nd ed., 1883.

J. de La Rocca, *Biographie de la famille Abbatucci*, 1857.

G. de Romand, *De l'état des partis en France*, 1839.

M. Rousselet, *La Magistrature sous la monarchie de juillet*, 1937.

P. Saint-Marc, *Émile Ollivier*, 1950.

R. Schnerb, *Rouher*, 1949.

S. R. Schram, *Protestantism and Politics in France*, Alençon, 1954.

C. Seignobos, *La Révolution de 1848 — Le second empire*, 1921, in Lavisse's *Histoire de la France contemporaine*.
Le Déclin de l'empire et l'établissement de la troisième république, 1921, in the same series.

N. Senior, *Conversations with Thiers*, 2 vols., 1878.

Comte Donatien de Sesmaisons, *Une Révolution doit avoir un terme*, 1816.

A. Siegfried, *Mes Souvenirs de la troisième république: mon père et son temps: Jules Siegfried, 1836–1922*, 1952.
Tableau politique de la France de l'ouest sous la troisième république, 1913.

A. Tardieu, *La Révolution à refaire*. Vol. 2: *La profession parlementaire*, 1937.

J. Taschereau, *Revue rétrospective ou archives secrètes du dernier gouvernement*, 1848.

Capt. Tattet, *Lettres inédites du maréchal Bugeaud*, 1923.

A. de Tocqueville, *Œuvres complètes d'Alexis de Tocqueville publiées par Mme de Tocqueville*, vols. 5-7, 1866.

A. Trannoy, *Le Romantisme politique de Montalembert avant 1843*, 1942.

J. Vidalenc, *Le Département de l'Eure sous la monarchie constitutionnelle*, 1952.
Les Demi-Soldes, 1955.

A. F. A. Vivien, *Études administratives*, 3rd ed., 2 vols., 1859.

G. Weill, *Le Journal*, 1934.

G. D. Weil, *Les Élections législatives depuis 1789*, 1895.

Bibliography

The most useful of the well-known books of reference are :

M. Block, *Dictionnaire de l'administration française*, ed. of 1891.

A. Robert, Bourloton and Cougny, *Dictionnaire des parlementaires français*, 5 vols., 1890 ff., commonly known as Robert et Cougny.

G. Vapereau, *Dictionnaire des contemporains*, at least 5 editions, the most useful being those of 1865, 1870 and 1880.

INDEX

Abbatucci, Paul Séverin, 28
Abstention in the election of 1852, 40-1
Albufera, L. N. Suchet, Duc d', 28, 59, 137-8
Andelarre, J. F. Jacquot-Rouhier, Marquis d', 33
André, C. E., 52
Arago family influence, 34
Arcy, A. A. M., Comte de Gouy d', 33
Argent de Deux Fontaines, C. M., Baron, 33
Aristocracy, Napoleon III and the, 10-11 ; Bonapartist attempts to convert the, 161 ; formation of a new, 165
Arjuzon, F. J. F. T., Comte d', 33
Army, as a preparation for politics, 56
Audiffret-Pasquier, Duc d', 142
Aumale, Duc d', son of Louis Philippe, 108
Aymé, J. G., 32

Balay de La Bertrandière, J. J., 31
Barante, A. G. Prosper Brugière, Baron de, 116
Barbentane, L. A. de R., Comte de, 33
Baroche, Pierre Jules (1802–70), minister, his influence in Versailles, 22, 52 ; his brother-in-law, 26 ; complaints to the emperor (1863), 118-19
Barristers, how they entered politics, 55 ; why many in opposition, 56
Barrot, Odilon, 116
Bavoux, Évariste, 33
Beausset-Roquefort, Marquis de, 35
Beauvau, Marc, Prince de, 28
Beauverger, A. E. P., Baron de, 28
Belliard, Jean, 28
Belmontet, Louis (1799–1879), Bonapartist poet and politician, 29 ; his difficulties in entering parlia-

ment, 30 ; his career, 60 ; Napoleon's letter to him, 60
Berryer, P. A., legitimist leader, 117
Bertrand, L. H., 33
Bertron, Adolphe, 'Humane Candidate', 89
Bidault, J. J., 33
Bigrel, T., 33
Billault, Adolphe (1805–63), president of the legislature (1852-4), minister of the Interior (1854-8 and 1859-60), minister without portfolio (1860-3), minister of State (1863) : made no money out of politics, 61 ; his career, 67 ; his social and political views, 67-8 ; his policy in the election of 1857, 68–71 ; letter on the result of the election of 1857, 75 ; policy concerning the mayors, 92 ; mentioned, 33, 52
Bocher, H. E., 142
Bois de Mouzilly, T. E., 31, 52
Boissy d'Anglas, J. G. T., Comte, 33, 53
Bonapartism, difficulty of keeping aristocrats of the first empire loyal to, 151 ; its theory on revolutions, 153 ; increase in strength during second empire, 154 ; traditional explanation of its growth inadequate, 155 ; how devotees were created by the prefects, 158-63 ; how it gained at the expense of the legitimists, 166-8
Bonapartist dynasties, 52, 161
Bonapartist party, between 1814 and 1848, 4-6 ; during the second republic, 7, 22-5 ; efforts to create a new party in 1852, 11-14 ; membership, 28-33 ; opinions, 46-51 ; progress during the second empire, 158-75
Bonapartists, and 'Napoleonists', 4-5 ; defeat of ultra-Bonapartists,

189

26 ; different types of, 28-30 ;
conservative, 46-8 ; 'democratic',
49 ; of the first empire, 166 ; of
the liberal empire, 142-51
Bordeaux, 41, 139
Boucaumont, M. L. A. (known as
Gustave), 55
Bouches-du-Rhône, legitimists in,
14, 37
Bouchetal-Laroche, P. C. R., 18, 29
Bourcier de Villers, C. J. B., Comte
de, 33
Bourgeoisie, Bonapartist efforts to
convert, 162
Bourlon, P. H. D., 28
Brame, Jules (1818–78), minister in
1870, 71, 131
Bravay, L. F., 97
Broglie, Albert, Prince, later Duc
de, 147
Broglie, Victor, Duc de, 142
Brunet-Denon, V. J., General
Baron, 29
Bryas, Eugène, Comte de, his politi-
cal career, 32
Bûcher de Chauvigné, Gustave, 33,
35
Buffet, Louis (1818–98), minister of
the second republic, the second
empire and the third republic,
opinion on the constitution (1857),
74 ; views in 1860, 107-9 ; election in 1863, 117 ; political
opinions and career, 145-7 ; his
amendment of 1866, 132-3
Buquet, H. A. L., Baron, 28
Busson-Billault, J. H., 52

Caffarelli, E. A., Comte de, 28
Calvet-Rogniat, F., 31
Calvière, C. F. M. A. J., Marquis
de, 33
Cambacérès, E. A. N., Comte de,
28, 52
Carayon-Latour, M. P. C. E., Baron
de, 33, 64
Carné, L. M., Comte de, 142
Carnot, L. H., minister of Educa-
tion in 1848, 73
Caruel de St-Martin, Paul, Baron, 32
Cassagnac, Adolphe de Granier de,
Bonapartist journalist and poli-
tician, how he became M.P., 30 ;
his career, 59 ; and Émile Ollivier,
124 ; his power in Gers, 165

Caulaincourt, Marquis de, 28
Cavaignac, General L. E., 73, 113
Chabrillan, L. O. T., Comte de, 28
Chambrun, J. D. A. de P., Comte
de, 59, 118, 132
Champagny, Napoléon, Comte de,
28
Chanterac, B. P. L., Comte de, 33
Charente, Bonapartism in, 165-6
Charlier, L. V., 31
Chasseloup-Laubat, Prosper, Mar-
quis de (1805–73), minister of
Marine and Colonies (1851 and
1860–7), minister of Algeria and
Colonies (1859–60), minister presi-
dent of the Council of State
(1869) : his financial integrity,
62 ; and the theory of the liberal
empire, 152 ; mentioned, 33
Chateaubriand on royalism, 8
Chauchard, J. B. H., Baron, 33
Chaumont-Quitry, O. C. J., Marquis
de, 81
Chazelles, P. L. B. de, 33
Cher, department of, Bonapartism
in, 29
Chevalier, Auguste (brother of Mi-
chel), 138
Chevalier, Michel, on the politics of
Hérault, 37
Chevandier de Valdrôme, J. P. E. N.
(1810–78), minister of the Interior
(1870), his career and opinions,
150-1
Chevreau, Henri, prefect and later
minister, letter to Billault, 98
Chevreau, J. H. (father of the pre-
fect), 29
Choque, E. L. J., 33
Civrac, M. H. L., Comte Durfort de,
33, 70-1
Clebsattel, A. de, 33
Clergy, 44, 69, 116, 141, 162
Committees, as a method of politi-
cal organisation, 22-5
Conneau, Dr. F. A. H. (1803–77),
Napoleon III's physician, 29, 30,
60
Conseil, A. B., 21, 31
Conservatives, 46-9
Corneille, P. A., descendant of the
poet, 52
Coup d'état, why impossible in 1869,
143
Crussol, Duc de, 142

THE END

PRINTED BY R. & R. CLARK, LTD., EDINBURGH